PRESENCE AND PRE-EXPRESSIVITY-2

Contemporary Theatre Review
1997, Vol. 7, Part 1, p. iii
Reprints available directly from the publisher
Photocopying permitted by license only

Contents

Contemporary Theatre Review
1997, Vol. 7, Part 1, pp. 1–10
Reprints available directly from the publisher
Photocopying permitted by license only

Body in Mind: Exploring Pre-Expressivity

Val Taylor

Since the Enlightenment, exploration of the processes and effects of the human psyche has provided much of the motor energy of Western dramatic writing. Reversing the Aristotelian order of priorities which gave pre-eminence to plot over character, late nineteenth and twentieth century plays have tended to give precedence to character over plot. Instead of situations revealing, or perhaps honing, the true inner nature of dramatic figures such as Oedipus or Antigone, it has (arguably) more often been the 'break-out' of a particular trait of character which has provoked, altered or fuelled the onset and subsequent development of situations in modern drama: *why* Hèdda Gabler burns Lövborg's manuscript, or Julie flirts with Jean, for example. The distinction is sometimes a fine one, but its impact upon the work of the modern Western actor has been immense.

Elevation of character to pre-eminent dramatic status coincided with the thrust of the Naturalistic movement towards mimetic reproduction of human behaviour: the perfect reflection of nature in the mirror of the stage. Character became thoroughly contextualised socially, politically, economically, in order to trace the 'shaping' of the psyche; which then entirely governed and accounted for his/her subsequent physical actions. It became the playwright's task, qua social anthropologist, to delineate clearly the details of, and the interaction between, both context and character. Correspondingly, the primary task of the modern actor became accurate mimicry of real human behaviour in the given fictive context: a collaboration between minute social observation and imaginative projection. The accuracy of both observation and projection was crucial to the success of such drama, the objective of which was the debating of the nature of the human psyche with the audience; and to facilitate such a debate, recognition, by the audience, of the motivating psychology underlying the behavioural phenomena of the character's physical actions and verbal utterances, was of paramount importance. The actor's ability to *express*, and the nature of that expression became critical factors.

Stanislavsky's experiments in actor training and performance praxis responded to this priority shift; their effectiveness in meeting the reconstituted task is attested by the continued pre-eminence, in Western theatre, of the System and its derivations. The primary objective in the System – its 'super-objective' – is *expressivity*, but with a particular focus. In a paper given at the Centre for Performance Research's conference on *Theatre, Anthropology and Theatre Anthropology* (1988), Franco Ruffini suggested that Stanislavsky's System is centred less on *individual* character psychology than upon the search for a form of psychology which would render the character's actions coherent and credible to actor and audience: a psychological profiling which actually tends towards typology. Ruffini suggested that the *innate psychology* of the character was its *pre-expressive* level; the subsequent actions and utterances which constitute the *given role* within the play, which may vary if the given role differs, must therefore be seen as the *expressive* level, according to this theory. The methods of the System – 'if'; given circumstances; emotion memory; truth and belief; units and objectives, etc. – being elements in the search for a coherent and credible psychology, must thus be seen as work done at the pre-expressive rather than the expressive level. It is work which first establishes not the uniqueness of the character's psyche, but its *common bases:* the character's individuality is generated within the surface structure – the expressive level. At the pre-expressive level, which must, by this light, be seen as the deep structure, the search for common bases – which I have suggested leads to the creation of types – offers the opportunity to make observations about human psychological identity in general.

The grouping of these methods under the heading of 'psychotechnique' makes it quite clear that these are mental techniques: whilst their effects may be acutely manifested in bodily sensations or emotional responses, their causal origins lie in mental processes. Shomit Mitter, in *Systems of Rehearsal*, identifies the centrality of mental processes in the System: "In the alchemy of drawing reality from representation, the actor's problem is primarily that of knowledge." [1] The 'problem' is therefore epistemological, and the System an epistemological exercise, the outcomes of which are behavioural phenomena. But the realistic drive of the System and the form of dramatic writing it serves offer not only an epistemology and a phenomenology, but also an ontology which both work to reveal. Thus Stanislavsky's System, while in itself constituting an epistemological exercise, bespeaks an underlying ontology. Following Ruffini, if expressivity is its epistemological goal

[1] Shomit Mitter, *Systems of Rehearsal: Stanislavsky, Brecht, Grotowski and Brook* (Routledge, 1992) p. 10.

then pre-expressivity may be considered its ontological base. And for Stanislavsky – and Ruffini on Stanislavsky – that ontology is rooted in the psyche.

Western naturalistic strategies are not, of course, the only ones available; nor were they, at the time of development of the System. The Biomechanical explorations of Meyerhold, provoked by his experience of the System under Stanislavsky, took a different tack. Instead of locating itself in mental processes, Meyerhold's work centred upon physical exercises ('études') as an emotional focus. Physical actions were dissected into a tripartite cycle: Intention, Realization, Refusal of the Action. This cycle was enacted in the form of continuous rhythmic movement, not, as has tended to be thought, a series of isolated, angular stages: more Martha Graham than robotics. [2] If we re-apply the terminology used in the context of the System, it would seem that the particular movements produced in Biomechanics may be deemed to occupy the expressive level. What then is the pre-expressive level? If it is the character's psychology under the System, under Biomechanics it is the character's physiology: his/her body, in motion. Once again, it is not the particularity of the individual body which is under investigation but the 'common body': the human body itself. It is, it seems, the physical (surface) variants, and the rhythmic cycle of movement each variant produces, which are the expressive manifestation of the pre-expressive (deep) level.

But complexity arises in identifying the ontological, epistemological and phenomenological levels. Certainly it seems possible to classify the particular visible movements in, say, Shooting The Bow, as phenomena; and to regard the dissection of those movements into the three-part cycle – the Étude – as epistemological in nature. If, as before, we locate the ontology within the pre-expressive level, and locate the pre-expressive level in Biomechanics in the human body-in-motion, then the ontology which Biomechanics addresses is thereby also located within the physical plane.

It is complex because of the fictive nature of drama itself. Would we consider drama an ontological or an epistemological exercise? Is it a conception of reality, or a procedure for revealing such a conception – a realism? As an innate human impulse (vide Aristotle) it might lay claim to ontological status; considering its varying styles, it must surely be epistemological in nature. The fictive nature of character psychology lends itself to this debate, through its connection to *actual* human psychology: for the latter is, I would suggest, itself an exercise in

[2] I am indebted to Dr. Valerie Lucas, Roehampton Institute, for a discussion of Meyerhold's Biomechanics following a conference with former practitioners of the Moscow Art Theatre Studio.

ontology. In this respect, the relationship of drama to the real world it addresses is clearer: if *human* psychology is the ontological site, then (fictive) *character* psychology is epistemological in nature.

The question of the *character's fictive body* is more complex. Whilst we are, in some naturalistic drama, given material indicators of the character's fictive body – Hedda's thin hair contrasted to the bushy vibrancy of Thea Elvsted's for example – delineation of the body of a character is much less detailed than delineation of the his/her psychology. What delineation there is tends to refer to the body's capacity for movement or activity – Firs' slowness, Yepihodov's clumsiness – or to certain physical states such as hunger or weariness. The under-writing of the fictive body means that the reader's sense of a character's body is subsumed beneath the welter of impressions of his/her personality. Thus, when we think of a character, it is predominantly the psychological profile we are considering; when we think in physical terms, it is often the *actor's body in performance* that we are remembering, eliding this with the *character's fictive body*. Hamlet's psychological profile is very familiar to us; his physical characteristics, however, tend to be those of famous actors of Hamlet: the blond hair and athleticism of Olivier, for example. In this sense, whilst we can *discuss* him endlessly, we cannot *describe* him physically.

Meyerhold's Biomechanics seem to me not so much to address the fictive body of the character, as the actor's body in performance; unlike Stanislavsky's System which seems primarily to address the fictive psychology of the character, rather than the actual psychology of the actor. (Lee Strasberg's variant upon the System, the 'Method', blurs this distinction.) Unlike human psychology, which, considering the divergence of psychoanalytic theories, I have argued is itself an ontological exercise, the human body is a reality: not a *conception* of reality, subject to interpretation, but the thing itself. The pre-expressive level of the character in Biomechanics is thus not the under-written *fictive* body, but the actor's *real* body: the reality, not the concept of the reality, the actual, not the ontological. The significant presence of the actor's real body onstage complicates immeasurably the question of ontology, epistemology and drama.

Perhaps this issue may be approached through the exploration of pre-expressivity, a level I have linked to the ontological in both Stanislavsky's and Meyerhold's work. Notions of pre-expressivity are relatively recent in the West, popularised predominantly through the investigations, writings and performances of groups such as Eugenio Barba's ISTA. It is not a new concept in Oriental and Asian theatres, whose forms and methods it seems always to have underpinned, as theatre anthropological research has shown. But what exactly is it? How is it to be defined? It seems to be a very loose and somewhat vague term, if the multiplicity of definitions in Barba and Nicola Savarese's 1991 *A Dictionary of Theatre Anthropology: The Secret Art of the Performer* is anything to go by: (my emphases)

> "The level which deals with how to render *the actor's energy* scenically alive, that is, with how the actor can become a *presence* which immediately attracts the spectator's attention, is the pre-expressive level." (p. 188)
>
> "The pre-expressive level ... is therefore an operative level ... a pragmatic category, a praxis, the aim of which ... is to strengthen *the character's scenic bios.*" (p. 188)
>
> "The pre-expressive principles ... also are based on a network of fictions ... 'magic ifs', which deal with the physical forces which move the body." (p. 19)
>
> "The pre-expressive level can be defined as the level at which *the performer* constructs and directs her *presence* on the stage, independent of and before her final goals and expressive results. 'Presence' in this definition ... is literal." (p. 64)

Of these four definitions, the first two are by Eugenio Barba and Nicola Savarese writing together; the third by Barba alone, and the fourth by Franco Ruffini. The first three show a definite tendency to refer to physicality and the body; Ruffini's occurs within the entry "Dilation", under the sub-heading "The Dilated Mind".

For the reader struggling to grasp what is pre-expressivity, and for the actor trying to uncover the 'praxis' alluded to, there seems to be a conflict of opinions as to whether it is the body or the mind which is the pre-expressive site. Or if it is both body and mind, how pre-expressivity functions in both, and how the two interrelate. The issue is compounded further by the fact that whilst the first and fourth definitions refer to the actor/performer, the second refers to the *character*; the third is unspecific which is meant. Perhaps we may begin to unravel the tangle if we note that the first and fourth refer to physical energy and physical presence – properties of the real body of the actor, whilst the second addresses the character's "scenic bios": the analogous energy which animates the 'presence' of the character's *fictive body*. The third seems to address the process by which this animation occurs: the actor's material presence and physical energy activated by his/her mental energy and presence, in service of the creation of the fictive mind and body of the character.

What seems to be suggested by all four definitions is a deliberate heightening of impact of the actor's reality, with the intention of drawing the attention of the audience to it. The character, it would appear, is generated within that heightened, or exaggerated, or 'excessive' condition. Perhaps it may be considered that in this heightened condition the actor is rendered more *significant* – in the sense of *intending to signify*, or simply *to mean*. Theatre semioticians have remarked on the signifying complexity of the actor on stage both as real human being, and also as icon. This complexity is attributed semiotically to the simple fact of being *on stage*, that is, *in performance*. Perhaps it is possible to see a connection between the heightening of significance given the actor by dint of being 'in performance', and the heightening which is the objective of work done at the pre-expressive level. In this sense, it may be suggested that pre-expressivity is not simply a set of techniques, or a means to an end, but a state: a charismatic condition.

The notion of charisma accrues to drama most often in the arena of popular culture: the concept of the *star* and his/her 'indefinable' *star quality*. It is frequently discussed within the context of the eroticisation or fetishisation of particular actors, (cf. Richard Dyer, *Stars*, for example) and linked to their capacity to excite desire in the audience. Such actors are often acknowledged as being able to 'turn on' or 'off', seemingly at will, their charismatic attraction: the famous anecdote of Marilyn Monroe, told by Susan Strasberg, is one such instance. If the connection between this kind of charisma and notions of pre-expressivity which I have suggested above, is tenable, then certain observations become possible. Far from being 'indefinable', it would seem that charisma may be attributable to the nature of performance itself, and the concomitant heightening of significance performance confers upon the actor-in-performance. Further if there is a link between performative significance and pre-expressivity, then charisma is itself pre-expressive, and techniques pertaining to work at the pre-expressive level will also by definition be charismatic techniques. The erotic roots of charisma in the evocation of desire likewise inform thinking about the nature of pre-expressivity: the pre-expressive condition becomes an eroticised condition, and its techniques may be seen as erotic techniques, creating the actor as an object of desire. My earlier comments concerning the identification of the pre-expressive level in the psyche (Stanislavsky) or in the body (Meyerhold) are also informed by this connection.

Shomit Mitter suggests [3] that Stanislavsky's psycho-techniques actually inhibited rather than freed the MAT actors: the intended progression from mental conception to physical realization became blocked by the sheer dominance of logic over emotional spontaneity. He notes that Stanislavsky sought a condition beyond the domain of conscious thought (intention?), a condition Stanislavsky termed 'inspiration'; and in order to achieve it, moved his actors from psycho-technique to somatic exercises: physical exercises generative of emotional responses. Franco Ruffini views the System, and the question of mental work, differently. [4] He identifies a need for a 'dilated' mind capable of provoking the actions

[3] Mitter, p. 15.

[4] Franco Ruffini, "The Dilated Mind" in Eugenio Barba and Nicola Savarese, *A Dictionary of Theatre Anthropology: The Secret Art of the Performer*, (Routledge, 1991) pp. 64–67.

of a similarly 'dilated' body. The source of 'dilation' resides in *excessive activity*, in both cases: that is, activity which both demands and produces an excess of energy. For Ruffini, the psycho-technical work of the System offers that excessive mental activity. He finds its value not to reside in the information gleaned from such intellectual investigations as 'if', or 'given circumstances', but in the activity of questioning itself: in the engagement with the task rather than in its conclusions – in the *thinking* rather than the thoughts. In this respect, he likens the System to the Socratic Method of instruction.

The 'dilated body', according to Barba and Savarese, [5] is also manifested in this quality of excess, and achievable through excessive activity – though not necessarily through excessive *motion*. Under headings such as "Theatre Anthropology", "Balance", "Dilation", "Oppositions", they identify the importance of a *compression of physical energy*, created by a contradictory *opposition of directed physical expressions*. This is not 'blocking' but rather a continuous process of contra-indications taking place within the body. For example, in "Balance", the everyday physical balance which distributes itself symmetrically throughout the body with the minimum expenditure of energy necessary to maintain it, is substituted, in pre-expressive work by an extraordinary play of related assymmetries – "equivalences" – which require great energy expenditure in order to maintain the new balance. This is termed 'precarious' or 'luxury balance' (p. 34). The maintenance of such a balance, or the succession of such balances in a movement sequence, is dynamised by the degree of energy utilised.

Movement is therefore an alternation of compressed and expressed energy: 'expressed', here, referring to directed and expended energy, in opposition to 'retained' energy. Such a movement is not, in and of itself, signifying: it is not *expressive*, as such. It is *pre*-expressive. The point of this physical work resides in the doing; in this, it corresponds to Ruffini's identification of the 'Socratic' value of Stanislavsky's System. It is a physical 'questioning'. There are similarities between this work and aspects of Meyerhold's Biomechanics: particularly the identification of the three-part cycle of movement.

The result of pre-expressive work on mind and body is the generation of a state which Barba terms 'incandescence', a kind of molecular excitation which produces, in physics, heat and light. The pre-expressive condition is thus an incandescent condition. The heightened appearance and sensations of such a condition are attention-grabbing: literally, attractive. If the pre-expressive condition is, as I have suggested earlier, also a charismatic one, then the linkage between pre-expressivity and

[5] Barba and Savarese, p. 203.

'incandescence' leads to the suggestion that the roots of charisma lie within that 'excessive' physical and mental excitation which generates that 'glow'. The erotic nature of charisma also informs our understanding of pre-expressive 'incandescence': it, too, seems rooted in desire. It seems that the attraction of the pre-expressive condition derives from the excess energy of the actor's heightened inhabitation of his/her sexuality.

Thinking further upon this, it is possible to see that this manifestation of the actor's sexuality is not primarily outwardly directed: that is, towards the audience. Such a directedness would be expressive in nature, and occurs *subsequently*, when the individualised surface variations are constructed. But this manifestation is *pre*-expressive, and therefore not yet outwardly directed: it is, instead, inwardly-directed, towards the 'common core' that I have argued is the site of pre-expressive work. It is the physical, mental and emotional experience of one's own reality as a sexual human being: a form of self-knowledge – or perhaps, following Ruffini, Barba and Savarese and the emphasis on process, a form of self-*knowing*. I am reminded of the importance, in feminist theory and practice, given to "writing the body" and the reclamation by women of their physical, emotional and psychic experience of their own sexuality. In this field, such explorations are a re-discovery of the individual's core identity, in the teeth of a perceived contradictory social identity; and a re-statement of the individual's participation in female sexual identity.

In this sense, perhaps it is possible to consider work at the pre-expressive level as more than simply work designed to enliven the actor's body and mind. If such enlivening also extends the actor's sense of his/her own sexual nature in a positive, invigorating fashion, then what is occuring is a particular experience of human identity: an ontological exploration. The particular techniques of pre-expressive work offer an epistemology, a means of revelation of the actor's perception of his/her sexual identity, and also a means of disclosing discrepancies between that and his/her social identity: between sex and gender. The movements, gestures and utterances arising from pre-expressive work, subsequently applied and directed at the expressive level, thus constitute phenomena; the study of which will enable the reconstruction of the ontology. From the feminist perspective, reconstruction of the underlying ontology may also serve to reveal the impact of a dominant, repressive ideology.

For me, this is most interesting about the concept of pre-expressivity. The writings of Barba and co. have come under fire from certain quarters of the feminist lobby, and rightly. In the assertion that the sex of the actor is irrelevant at the pre-expressive level, a particular concept of reality is promoted, which devalues the importance of human sexual identity. It suggests a kind of essentialism which denies sexual difference: a premise which feminist thinking rejects as ideologically-based. But I have not begun from this premise of absence of sexual difference. I have found, within pre-expressivity, an opportunity for *experiencing* difference in sexual identity for the actor, possibly free of the inflections of gender. Or, if such inflection is inescapable, then at least these pre-expressive techniques may be a means of disclosing them *as* gendered.

The emphasis in pre-expressive work on the equal importance of the body is critical. As I have earlier remarked, the body of the actor is the 'ground zero' of reality in performance, and dominates the audience's sense of the character's fictive body. The physical 'discourse' of sex and gender which the actor thus encapsulates also extends to the character's fictive body – which is, as I have said, frequently underwritten by the modern playwright. The intense concentration of modern writing upon the psychological profile of the character can often obscure the extent to which that profile is gender-inflected; an obscurity which is, I think, reinforced by the relative weakness of the delineation of the fictive body. Work in rehearsal which is wholly focussed upon the expressive level may tend to lead the actor to construct the character's physicality solely in terms of that inflected psychological profile. Work at the pre-expressive level may help to interrogate the psychology of the character in a productive manner, by disclosing the degree of inflection present. This is not because the actor experiences the *character's* sexuality, but because s/he re-experiences his/her *own*.

If pre-expressivity is a charismatic condition, then it is also an eroticised condition. For both actor and audience, the question of sexuality is inextricably linked to the *expression and reception* of sexuality, and to the issue of desire. The 'incandescent' pre-expressive actor is intentionally attractive to the audience; this attraction will be experienced, at some level, as desire. The issue of sexuality and gender inflection is therefore complicated by the impact of desire; as feminist film criticism has addressed in respect of the male and female 'gaze'. I think it is possible that exploration of the actor's work on pre-expressivity may be of considerable value to this area of discussion, by dint of its ability to operate at the ontological *and* epistemological levels.

But there is another area to which exploration of pre-expressivity may contribute, and that is in playwriting. As I noted at the outset, the development of modern writing has been in the domain of character psychology, at the expense of meeting the challenge of 'writing the (fictive) body'. Writing the fictive body has tended to mean writing external details of the *individual* body, and has lent itself to gender-inflection. There has been little conception of the body itself, at the 'deep-structural' level, except in the realm of feminist writing. Pre-expressivity and its attendant techniques may be able to offer a point of entry for a broader group of writers. And it seems likely that the potentially enhanced understanding of sexual identity may lead to a different, and more substantial, writing of the character's fictive body. This, in turn, may develop in alternative ways the writing of character in toto – physicality *and* psychology – and may impact very productively upon the perceived weaknesses of so-called 'physical theatre'.

Contemporary Theatre Review
1997, Vol. 7, Part 1, pp. 11–23
Reprints available directly from the publisher
Photocopying permitted by license only

Peter Brook and Traditional Thought

Basarab Nicolescu
Translated by David Williams

Dr. Nicolescu is a theoretical physicist, specialising in the theory of elementary particles, at the Centre National de la Recherche Scientifique in Paris. He is the author of numerous scientific articles published in international journals and reviews, as well as being a contributor to a number of research compilations. For a number of years, Dr. Nicolescu has been interested in the relationship between art, science and traditional thought. In 1968, he published a book discussing the interface between mathematics and poetry. Since 1978, he has been a member of the advisory editorial panel of the interdisciplinary review, *3ème Millénaire.*

The following extract is taken from an essay originally published in French in *Les Voies de la Création Théâtrale, Vol. XIII: Peter Brook* (ed. Georges Banu), Editions du C.N.R.S., 1985. The translation is by David Williams.

The first part of the essay (not reproduced here for reasons of space) identifies the link between theatre and 'Tradition' (in the sense of a body of information or set of practices, rather than 'mummification' or preservation) as a condition of "vital immediacy". Brook sees this as a "materiality of energy" which Nicolescu compares to an 'event' in the quantum mechanical sense, speculating that the information-exchange which enriches the spectator with a 'feeling of vitality' occurs, as in Gurdjieff's scientific systems theory, when systems are mutually open to each other; and such key moments represent a special kind of meaning richer than that to which rational thought has access.

[Editor's note]

Theatre, Determinism and Spontaneity

How can discipline and spontaneity be made to coexist and interact? Where does spontaneity come from? How can one distinguish true spontaneity from a simple automatic response, associated with a set of pre-existing (if unconscious) cliches? In other words, how can one differentiate between an association – perhaps unexpected, but nonetheless mechanical – with its source in what has been seen already, and the emergence of something really new?

Spontaneity introduces an *indeterminate* element into an evolutionary process. Heisenberg's celebrated 'uncertainty relation', or 'uncertainty principle', indicates that spontaneity is effectively active in nature. This principle tells us that the product of an increase in quantity of a quantum event's momentum through its spatial extension, or the product of an increase in energy through its temporal extension must be superior to a certain constant representing the elementary quantum of action. So if one were to ask, for example, for a precisely pinpointed *spatial* localisation of the quantum event, the result would be an infinite increase on the level of uncertainty of momentum: just as if one were to ask for a precisely pinpointed *temporal* localisation, the result would be an infinite increase on the level of energy. There is no need for a high degree of sophistication in mathematics or physics to understand that this signifies the impossibility of a precise localisation in space-time of any quantum event. The concept of *identity* in a classical particle (identity defined in relation to the particle itself, as a part separate from the Whole) is therefore necessarily smashed apart.

The quantum event is not made up of wave or particle, it is simultaneously wave and particle. The impossibility of precisely locating a quantum event in space-time can be understood as a consequence of the in-separability of events. Their 'aleatory' or 'probabilist' character does not reflect the action of 'chance'. The aleatory quantum is constructive, it has a direction – that of the self-organisation of natural systems. At the same time, the observer ceases to be an 'observer' – s/he becomes, as Wheeler has said, 'a participant'. Quantum theory has its place in the 'Valley of Astonishment' (one of the seven valleys in *Conference of the Birds*) where contradication and indeterminacy lie in wait for the traveller.

One could postulate the existence of a *general principle of uncertainty*, active in any process in reality. It is also necessarily active in theatrical space, above all in the relationship between audience and play. In the 'formula' for theatre suggested by Brook ('Theatre = Rra': 'Répétition', 'représentation', 'assistance'), [1] the presence – 'assistance' – of an audience plays an essential role:

'The only thing that all forms of theatre have in common is the need for an audience. This is more than a truism: in the theatre the audience completes the steps of creation.' [2]

[1] Peter Brook, *The Empty Space*, Harmondsworth, Penguin Books, 1977, p. 154.

[2] *Ibid*., p. 142. (*Translator's note* – On a literal level, the three French words in Brook's formula above mean *rehearsal*, *performance* and *attendance*, although they also suggest some of the connotations the same words have in English: e.g. rehearsal as an unglamorous repetitive process, performance as re-presentation etc. ... Brook plays on this tension).

The audience is part of a much greater unity, subject to the principle of uncertainty: 'It is hard to understand the true function of spectator, there and not there, ignored and yet needed. The actor's work is never for an audience, yet always is for one'. [3] The audience makes itself open to the actors, in its desire to 'see more clearly into itself', [4] and so the performance begins to act more fully on the audience. By opening itself up, the audience in turn begins to influence the actors, if the quality of their perception allows interaction. That explains why the global vision of a director can be dissolved by an audience's presence: the audience exposes the non-conformity of this vision with the structure of the theatrical event. The theatrical event is indeterminate, instantaneous, unpredictable, even if it necessitates the reunion of a set of clearly determined conditions. The director's role consists of working at great length and in detail to prepare the actors, thus enabling the emergence of the theatrical event. All attempts to *anticipate* or *predetermine* the theatrical event are doomed to failure: the director cannot substitute him/herself for the audience. The triangle comprising 'inner life of the actors – their relations with their partners – the audience's consciousness' can only be engendered at the actual moment of performance. The collective entity that is the audience makes the conciliatory element indispensable to the birth of the theatrical event: '(An audience's) true activity can be invisible, but also indivisible'. [5]

However invisible it is, this active participation by the audience is nonetheless material and potent: 'When the Royal Shakespeare Company's production of *King Lear* toured through Europe, the production was steadily improving ... The quality of attention that this audience brought expressed itself in silence and concentration: a feeling in the house that affected the actors as though a brilliant light were turned on their work'. [6] So it is evident why Brook's research work tends towards' ... a necessary theatre, one in which there is only a practical difference between actor and audience, not a fundamental one'. [7] The space in which the interaction between audience and actors takes place is infinitely more subtle than that of ideas, concepts, prejudices or preconditioning. The quality of the attention of both audience and actors enables the event to occur as a full manifestation of spontaneity. Ideally this interaction can transcend linguistic and cultural barriers. The C.I.R.T. actors

[3] *Ibid.*, p. 57.
[4] *Ibid.*, p. 152.
[5] *Ibid.*, p. 144.
[6] *Ibid.*, p. 25.
[7] *Ibid.*, p. 150.

can communicate just as well with African villagers, Australian aborigines or the inhabitants of Brooklyn; 'Theatre isn't about narrative. Narrative isn't necessary. Events will make the whole'.[8]

Many of the confusions concerning the problem of 'spontaneity' appear to have their source in a linear, mono-dimensional conception of the theatrical event. One can easily believe in the existence of laws such as *johakyu,* but that is insufficient in understanding how a theatrical event can take place through the *transition* between the different elements of *johakyu.* If one limits oneself to a strictly horizontal view of the action of *johakyu* (*jo,* the beginning: *ha,* the development: *kyu,* the ending), it is impossible to understand how one might arrive, for example, at the ultimate refinement of the *ha* part of *ha,* or to a paroxystic peak in the *kyu* part of *kyu.* What can produce the dynamic 'shocks' necessary for the movement not to stop, not to become blocked? How can the necessary continuity of a theatrical performance be reconciled with the discontinuity inherent in its different components? How can one harmonise the progression of the play, the actors' work and the perception liberated in the audience?

In other words, horizontal movement is meaningless by itself. It remains on the same level forever, no information is forthcoming. This movement only acquires a significance if it is combined with an *evolutionary* dynamic. It is as if each phenomenon in reality were subject, at every moment, to two contradictory movements, in two opposing directions: one ascending, the other descending. As if there were two parallel rivers, flowing with considerable force in two opposing directions: in order to pass from one river to the other, an external intervention – a 'shock' – is absolutely essential. This is where the full richness of the significance of the notion of 'discontinuity' is revealed.

But in order for this 'shock' to be effective, a certain concordance or overlap must exist between the 'shock' (which in itself is subject to the law of *johakyu*) and the system upon which it is acting. Therefore it becomes clear why each element of *johakyu* must be composed in turn of the three other elements – in other words, why there has to be a *jo-ha-kyu* sequence within the *jo,* the *ha* and the *kyu.* These different components enable interaction between the different systems to take place.

Therefore, in order for a harmonious movement to appear, a new dimension must be present: *johakyu* is not only active horizontally, but also vertically. If each element (*jo, ha* and *kyu*) is composed in turn of three other elements, therefore we obtain *nine* elements, two of which represent a sort of 'interval'. One of these is filled by the 'shock' enabling

[8] John Heilpern, *Conference of the Birds, The Story of Peter Brook in Africa,* Harmondsworth, Penguin, 1979, p. 165.

the horizontal transition to take place, the other by the 'shock' enabling the vertical transition to take place. In this way, one ends up with a vision of the action of Zeami's *johakyu* which is very close to the precise mathematical formulation Gurdjieff elaborated for his 'law of Seven' or 'octave law'. [9]

When one considers this two-dimensional vision of the action of *johakyu*, Peter Brook's insistence on the audience's central role in a theatrical event becomes clearer. The audience can follow the suggestions proposed to it by the playtext, the actors and the director. The first interval – between *jo* and *ha* – can be traversed by means of a more or less automatic exchange, the play can continue its horizontal movement. But the audience also has its own irreducible presence: its culture, its sensitivity, its experience of life, its quality of attention, the intensity of its perception. A 'resonance' between the actors' work and the audience's inner life can occur. Therefore the theatrical event can appear fully spontaneous, by means of vertical exchange – which implies a certain degree of will and of awareness – thereby leading to something truly new, not pre-existent in theatrical performance. The ascent of the action of *johakyu* towards the play's summit – the *kyu* of *kyu* – can therefore take place. The second interval is filled by a true 'shock', allowing the paradoxical coexistence of continuity and discontinuity.

We have described what could be considered to be a first level of perception in a theatre event. This analysis could be further refined by taking into account the tree-like structure (it is never ending) of *johakyu*. Different levels of perception, structured hierarchically in a qualitative 'ladder', could be discovered in this way. There are degrees of spontaneity, just as there are degrees of perception. The 'quality' of a theatrical performance is determined by the effective presence of these degrees.

We have also referred to a vertical dimension in the action of *johakyu*. This dimension is associated with two possible impulses: one ascending (evolution), the other descending (entropic involution). The ascending curve corresponds to a densification of energy, reflecting the tendency towards unity in diversity and an augmentation of awareness. It is in this sense that we have described the action of *johakyu* until this point.

But one might well conceive of a *johakyu in reverse*, such as appears, for example, in the subject of Peter Brook's film *Lord of the Flies*, where one witnessed the progressive degradation of a paradise towards a hell. An ideal, innocent space exists nowhere. Left to themselves, without the

---

[9] According to Gurdjieff, the number of fundamental laws, which regulate every process in the world and in mankind, is very restricted. In his cosmology, the fundamental laws are 'the law of Three' and 'the law of Seven', described in exhaustive detail in P. D. Ouspensky's *Fragments d'un enseignement inconnu*, Paris, Stock, 1978.

intervention of 'conscience' and 'awareness', the 'laws of creation' lead inexorably towards fragmentation, mechanicity and, in the final instance, to violence and destruction. In this way spontaneity is metamorphosed into mechanicity.

It should be noted that 'spontaneity' and 'sincerity' are closely linked. The usual moral connotation of 'sincerity' signifies its reduction to an automatic functioning based on a set of ideas and beliefs implanted into the collective psyche in an accidental way through the passage of time. In this sense, 'sincerity' comes close to a lie, in relation to itself. By ridding ourselves of the ballast of what does not belong to us, we can eventually become 'sincere': recognising laws, seeing oneself, opening oneself to relationships with others. Such a process demands work, a significant degree of effort: 'sincerity must be learnt'.[10] In relation to our usual conception of it, this kind of 'sincerity' resembles 'insincerity': 'With its moral overtones, the word (sincerity) causes great confusion. In a way, the most powerful feature of the Brecht actors is the degree of their *insincerity*. It is only through detachment that an actor will see his own cliches'.[11] The actor inhabits a double space of false and true sincerity, the most fruitful movement being an oscillation between the two: 'The actor is called upon to be completely involved while distanced – detached without detachment. He must be sincere, he must be insincere: he must practice how to be insincere with sincerity and how to lie truthfully. This is almost impossible, but it is essential ...'.[12]

The actor's predicament is reminiscent of Arjuna's perplexity when confronted with the advice that Krishna gives him, in the *Bhagavad Gita*, to reconcile action and non-action: paradoxically, action undertaken with understanding becomes interwined with inaction.

At every moment, the actor is confronted with a choice between acting and not-acting, between an action visible to the audience and an invisible action, linked to his/her inner life. Zeami drew our attention to the importance of intervals of non-interpretation or '*non-action*', separating a pair of gestures, actions or movements:

'It is a spiritual concentration which will allow you to remain on your guard, retaining all of your attention, at that moment when you stop dancing or chanting, or in any other circumstances during an *interval* in the text or in the mimic art. The emotion created by this inner spiritual concentration – which manifests itself externally – is what produces *interest* and enjoyment ... It is in relation to the degree of *non-consciousness* and selflessness, through a mental attitude in which one's spiritual

[10] P. D. Ouspensky, *Fragments ...*, op. cit., p. 216.
[11] Peter Brook, *The Empty Space*, op. cit., p. 130.
[12] *Ibid.*, p. 131.

reality is hidden even from oneself, that one must forge the link between what precedes and what follows the intervals of *non-action*. That is what constitutes the inner strength which can serve to reunite all ten thousand means of expression in the oneness of the spirit'.[13]

It is only by mastering the attitudes and associations produced in this way that the actor can truly 'play parts', putting him/herself in others' places. 'At every moment', wrote Gurdjieff, 'associations change automatically, one evoking another, and so on. If I am in the process of playing a part, I must be in control all the time. It is impossible to start again with the given impulse'.[14] In a sense a free man is one who can truly 'play parts'.

In the light of all that has been said so far in this essay, would it not now be possible to state that there is a very strong relationship between theatrical and spiritual work? Whether one agrees or not, a clear and important distinction between theatre research and traditional research must be made in order to avoid the source of an indefinite chain of harmful confusions, which in any case have already coloured certain endeavours in the modern theatre.

Traditional research addresses itself to man [sic] as a whole, calling into play a wide range of aspects, infinitely richer than that of theatre research: after all, the latter's end is aesthetic. Traditional research is closely linked with an oral teaching, untranslatable into ordinary language. Isn't it significant that no traditional writings ever describe the process of self-initiation? In his 'Third Series', faced with the impossibility of the task, Gurdjieff preferred to destroy his manuscript – what was eventually published as *Life is real only then, when 'I am'* is only a collection of fragments from that manuscript. On several occasions, Saint John of the Cross announced a treatise on the 'mystical union', but no trace has ever been found of such a work. Finally, 'Attar devoted the major part of his poem *Conference of the Birds* to the story of the discussions between the birds and a description of the preparation for their journey: the journey itself and the meeting with the Simorgh only take up a few lines.

Theatre research clearly has another end in mind: art, theatre. Peter Brook himself has strongly emphasised the need for such a distinction: *'theatre work is not a substitute for a spiritual search'*.[15] In itself theatrical

[13] Zeami, *La tradition secrète du No*, Paris, Gallimard, 1960, p. 131. (*Translator's note* – Perhaps the most useful of English translations available, both in this instance and elsewhere, is *On the Art of the No Drama: The Major Treatises of Zeami*, trans. J. Thomas Rimer and Yamazaki Masakazu, New Jersey, Princeton University Press, 1984. See 'Connecting all the arts through one intensity of mind', from 'A mirror held to the Flower', p. 230. 96–97).

[14] G. I. Gurdjieff, *Gurdjieff parle à ses élèves*, Paris, Stock/Monde ouverte, 1980, p. 230.

[15] A. C. H. Smith, *Orghast at Persepolis*, London, Eyre Methuen, 1972, p. 251.

experience is insufficient to transform the life of an actor. Nevertheless, like a savant, for example, or indeed any human being, the actor can experience *fleetingly* what could be 'a higher level of evolution'. Theatre is an imitation of life, but an imitation based upon the concentration of energies released in the creation of a theatre event. So one can become aware, on an experiential level, of the full richness of the present moment. If theatre is not really the decisive meeting with oneself and with others, it nonetheless allows for a certain degree of exploration to take place.

This fundamental ambiguity recurs in Grotowski's approach, at least such as it is described by Brook: 'The theatre, he believes, cannot be an end in itself: like dancing or music in certain dervish orders, the theatre is a vehicle, a means for self-study, self-exploration ... '.[16] According to Brook's conception of the theatre, it cannot lay claim to unity, in terms of its end. Of course one can arrive at certain privileged moments; 'At certain moments, this fragmented world comes together, and for a certain time it can rediscover the marvel of organic life. The marvel of being one'.[17] But theatre work is ephemeral, subject to the influences (both evoluted and involuted) of the environment. This impermanence prevents it from leading to 'points of dynamic concentration'. In answer to a question about *Orghast*, Brook replied that theatre work is –

> '... self-destructive within waves ... You go through lines and points. The line that has gone through *Orghast* should come to a point, and the point should be a work ... obviously there is a necessary crystallising of the work into a concentrated form. It's always about that – coming to points of concentration.'[18]

On the Possibility of a Universal Language

When A. C. H. Smith asked him about the possibility of a 'universal language', Peter Brook dismissed the question as being meaningless.[19] His response reflects a fear of the stifling of a vital question by endless theoretical considerations, by deforming and maimimg abstractions. How many prejudices and cliches are unleashed automatically simply by pronouncing the two words 'universal language'? And yet Brook's entire work testifies to his search for a new language which endeavours to unite sound, gesture and word, and in this way to free meanings which could not be expressed in any other way. But above all this research is

[16] Peter Brook, *The Empty Space*, op. cit., p. 66.
[17] A. C. H. Smith, *Orghast at Persepolis*, op. cit., p. 52.
[18] *Ibid.*, p. 264.
[19] *Ibid.*, pp. 255–256.

experimental: something living emerges into the theatre space, and it matters little what name one gives to it. 'What happens', Brook asks, 'when gesture and sound turn into word? What is the exact place of the word in theatrical expression? As vibration? Concept? Music? Is any evidence buried in the structure of certain ancient languages?'.[20]

The fact that, by themselves, words cannot provide total access to reality has been well known for a long time. In the final analysis, any definition of words by words is based on indefinite terms. Where does linguistic determinism begin, and where does it end? Can it be characterised by a single value, by a finite number of values or by an infinite number? And if, according to Korzybski's famous phrase, 'the map is not the territory',[21] it nevertheless has the considerable advantage of a structure similar to that of the territory. How can this similarity become operative? 'The word is a small visible portion of a gigantic unseen formation', writes Brook.[22] Starting with this 'small visible portion', how can one gain access to the 'gigantic formation' of the universe as a whole? A theatrical event, as has already been suggested, determines the appearance of a laddered structure of different levels of perception. How can any single word encapsulate the sum of these levels?

The relativisation of perception has enabled us to specify a phenomenon's place in reality, as well as how it is linked to the rest. A word, a gesture, an action are all linked to a certain level of perception, but, in the true theatrical event, they are also linked to other levels present in the event. Relativity allows us to uncover the *invariance* concealed behind the multiplicity of forms of phenomena in different systems of reference. This vision of things is close to that implied by the 'principle of relativity' formulated by Gurdjieff.[23]

Relativity conditions vision: without relativity there can be no vision. The playwright who takes his/her own reality for reality as a whole presents an image of a dessicated and dead world, in spite of any 'originality' that he/she might have shown. 'Unfortunately the playwright rarely searches to relate their detail to any larger structure – it is as though they accept without question their intuition as complete, their reality as all of reality.'[24] Death itself can be relativised in an acceptance of contradiction. Brook cites the example of Chekhov: 'In Chekhov's work, death is omnipresent ... But he learnt how to balance compassion with distance ... This awareness of death, and of the precious moments

[20] *Ibid.*, p. 42.

[21] Alfred Korzybski, *Science and Sanity*, Lakeville, Connecticut, The International Non-Aristotelian Publishing Co., 1958, p. 58.

[22] Peter Brook, *The Empty Space*, op. cit., p. 15.

[23] P. D. Ouspensky, *Fragments ...*, op. cit., p. 111.

[24] Peter Brook, *The Empty Space*, op. cit., p. 40.

that could be lived, endow his work with a sense of the relative: in other words, a viewpoint from which the tragic is always a bit absurd'.[25] Non-identification is another word for vision.

Theatre work can be the constant search for a simultaneous perception, by both actors and audience, of every level present in an event. Brook describes his own research in this concise formulation:

> 'the simple relationship of movement and sound that passes directly, and the single element which has the ambiguity and density that permits it to be read simultaneously on a multitude of levels – those are the two points that the research is all about.'[26]

The principle of relativity clarifies what an eventual 'universal language' could be. For Gurdjieff, this new, precise, mathematical language had to be centred around the idea of evolution: 'The fundamental property of this new language is that *all* ideas are concentrated around *one single* idea: in other words, they are all considered, in terms of their mutual relationships, from the point of view of a single idea. And this idea is that of *evolution*. Not at all in the sense of a *mechanical* evolution, naturally, because that does not exist, but in the sense of a conscious and voluntary evolution. It is the only possible kind .... The language which permits understanding is based on the knowledge of its place in the evolutionary ladder'.[27] So the *sacred* itself could be understood to be anything that is linked to an evolutionary process.

This new language involves the participation of body and emotions. Human beings in their totality, as an image of reality, could therefore forge a new language. We do not only live in the world of action and reaction, but also in that of spontaneity and of self-conscious thought.

Traditional symbolic language prefigures this new language. When talking about different systems which convey the idea of unity, Gurdjieff said:

> 'A symbol can never be taken in a definitive and exclusive sense. In so far as it express the laws of unity in indefinite diversity, a symbol itself possesses an indefinite number of aspects from which it can be considered, and it demands from whoever approaches it the capacity to see it from different points of view. Symbols that are transposed into the words of ordinary language harden, become less clear: they can quite easily become their own opposites, imprisoning meaning within dogmatic and narrow frame-works, without even permitting the relative freedom of a logical examination of the subject. Reason merely provides a literal understanding of symbols, only ever attributing to them a single meaning.'[28]

---

[25] Peter Brook, in the programme for *La Cerisaie*, Paris, C.I.C.T., 1981, p. 110.

[26] A. C. H. Smith, *Orghast at Persepolis*, op. cit., p. 248.

[27] P. D. Ouspensky, *Fragments ...*, op. cit., p. 112.

[28] *Ibid.*, pp. 400–401.

The fact that a symbol possesses an indefinite number of aspects does not mean that it is imprecise at all. Indeed it is its reading on an indefinite number of levels which confers on it its extreme precision. Commenting on the theatre of Samuel Beckett, Brook writes:

'Beckett's plays are symbols in an exact sense of the word. A false symbol is soft and vague: a true symbol is hard and clear. When we say 'symbolic' we often mean something drearily obscure: a true symbol is specific, it is the only form a certain truth can take ... We get nowhere if we expect to be told what they mean, yet each one has a relation with us we can't deny. If we accept this, the symbol opens in us a great wondering O.'[29]

It is clear therefore why Brook believes Chekhov's essential quality to be 'precision', and why he states that today '... fidelity is the central concern, an approach which necessitates weighing every single word and bringing it into sharp focus'.[30] Only then can words have an influence: they can become active, bearers of real significance, if the actor behaves as a 'medium', allowing words to act through and 'colour' him/her, rather than him/her trying to manipulate them.[31]

By forgetting relativity, language has become in time inevitably narrower, diminished in its emotional and even intellectual capacities. It has been necessarily 'bastardised': one word is taken for another, one meaning for another. The *Orghast* experiment showed in a startling way that a return to an *organic* language, detached from the dread bonding of abstraction to abstraction, is possible. Words invented by the poet Ted Hughes and fragments performed in different ancient languages acted as catalysts to the reciprocal transformation between movement and sound, as an expression of an inner state, meaning no longer needing to be filtered solely through cerebral activity. In an interview with *American Theatre*, Brook emphasised that 'actors, whatever their origin, can play intuitively a work in its original language. This simple principle is the most unusual thing that exists in the theatre ...'.[32]

Evidently the relativisation of perception demands hard work, a considerable effort, an inner *silence* that is a sort of penitence. Silence plays an integral part in Brook's work, beginning with the research into the inter-relationship of silence and duration with his Theatre of Cruelty group in 1964, and culminating in the rhythm punctuated with silences that is indefinably present at the core of his film *Meetings with Remarkable Men*: 'In silence there are many potentialities: chaos or order, muddle or

[29] Peter Brook, *The Empty Space*, op. cit., pp. 64–65.

[30] Peter Brook, in the programme for *La Cerisaie*, op. cit., pp. 107–108.

[31] A. C. H. Smith, *Orghast at Persepolis*, op. cit., p. 27.

[32] Peter Brook, interview published in *American Theatre, 1970–1971*: quoted in A. C. H. Smith *Orghast at Persepolis*, op. cit., p. 40.

pattern, all lie fallow – the invisible-made-visible is of sacred nature ...'.[33] Silence is all-embracing, and it contains countless 'layers'.[34]

One could suggest that events and silence constitute the fabric of any theatre performance. Silence comes at the end of action, as in *Conference of the Birds*: 'A beautiful symbolic opposition is drawn between the black of the mourning material and the hues of the puppets. Colour disappears, all sparkle is suppressed, silence is established', observes Georges Banu.[35] The richness of silence confuses, embarrasses and disturbs, and yet it is joy that is hidden within it, that 'strange irrational joy' that Brook detected in the plays of Samuel Beckett.[36]

It is no coincidence that the words 'empty space' form the title of one of the two books on theatre Brook has ever published. One must create an emptiness, a silence within oneself, in order to permit the growth of reality's full potentiality. This is what Tradition has always taught us.

Is silence the premonitory sign of a true 'universal language'? In a passage in *The Empty Space*, Brook writes: '... everything is a language for something and nothing is a language for everything'.[37] Is this 'nothing' – 'formless', 'bottomless', as Jacob Böhme called it – the basis of all form, process and event? And how can one reconcile this infinitely rich, formless silence with aesthetic form, other than through incessant search, continual investigation and pitiless questioning, relentlessly pursued along a cutting edge? Perhaps it is above all 'tightropes' that are missing from contemporary artistic research:

> 'We can try to capture the invisible, but we must not lose touch with common sense ... The model as always is Shakespeare. His aim continually is holy, metaphysical, yet he never makes the mistake of staying too long on the highest plane. He knew how hard it is for us to keep company with the absolute – so he continually bumps us down to earth ... We have to accept that we can never see all of the invisible. So after straining towards it, we have to face defeat, drop down to earth, then start up again.'[38]

Peter Brook is the only one to follow the path he has chosen. On such a path, there can be neither 'sources' nor absolute 'models'.

If one accepts Korzybski's suggestion,[39] the history of human thought can be roughly divided into three periods, adopting as the basis for classification the relationship between the observer and what is observed. In

[33] Peter Brook, *The Empty Space*, op. cit., p. 64.

[34] *Ibid.*, p. 29.

[35] Georges Banu, '*La Conférence des Oiseaux*, ou le chemin vers soi-même', in *Les Voies de La Création Théâtrale*, vol. X, Paris, C.N.R.S., 1982, p. 285.

[36] Peter Brook, *The Empty Space*, op. cit., p. 66.

[37] *Ibid.*, p. 133.

[38] *Ibid.*, p. 69.

[39] Alfred Korzybski, *Science and Sanity*, op. cit., p. 99.

the first period ('pre-scientific'), the observer is everything, while what is being observed has little or no importance. In the second period ('classical' or 'semi-scientific'), what is observed comprises the only important aspect: this 'classical' materialist tendency continues to dominate most areas of concern today. Finally, in the third period ('scientific' – still embryonic at the present time), a period in which Peter Brook seems to us to be one of the boldest explorers, gradually it becomes clear that knowledge results from a unity between the observer and what is observed. An encounter with Tradition can only enrich and ennoble this conception of unity. For the theatre, such a meeting is not abstract or intellectual, but experimental. One could even suggest that theatre is a privileged field of study of Tradition.

At the end of this essay, perhaps one must confess that it seems impossible to approach Brook's theatre work from a theoretical point of view. All that we can offer is a 'reading', one of a multitude of other possibilities. In *The Empty Space*, Brook writes:

> 'Most of what is called theatre anywhere in the world is a travesty of a word once full of sense. War or peace, the colossal bandwagon of culture trundles on, carrying each artist's traces to the evermounting garbage heap ... We are too busy to ask the only vital question which measures the whole structure: why theatre at all? what for? ... Has the stage a real place in our lives? What function can it have? What could it serve?'[40]

The question is still being asked.

[40] Peter Brook, *The Empty Space*, op. cit., pp. 45–46.

Contemporary Theatre Review
1997, Vol. 7, Part 1, pp. 25–34
Reprints available directly from the publisher
Photocopying permitted by license only

Grotowski, Holiness and the Pre-Expressive

Ralph Yarrow

I think people in the West are whole-seeking in ways and on a scale not experienced in our culture for hundreds of years.

Richard Schechner

The theatrical and paratheatrical activity of Jerzy Grotowski is described in a number of texts which employ fairly overtly religious discourse, including the concept of the *via negativa*. The intention behind his practice is to instigate a wholeness or holiness of physical and psychological functioning in performers and spectators. This essay discusses the methods and processes Grotowski uses, and in so doing places them in the framework of ideas about "pre-expressivity", "presence" and "score", whilst also attempting to evaluate both the role of the cultural contexts in which Grotowski has operated and the outcomes of his work.

To what extent is the texture of Grotowski's activity constructed by the rhetoric evident in his writing, or does it offer a "liberation" from habitual forms of behaviour and production of meaning? To what extent is theatre "holy" for Grotowski and other major 20th century practitioners? What does Grotowski mean by this term? Does he use it in the conventional religious sense, or is he trying to question or revise it? What changes occur as a result of his practice in performers and in the nature of the theatrical event?

Is this condition of holiness cognate with or related to Barba's "pre-expressivity", or some extension of it? Is it applicable both to performers and receivers? What kind of psychophysical or psychobiological condition are we talking about? What are its effects? Why should it have been particularly sought after in the period 1960–1990? Why do accounts and explanations of it tend to make use of Oriental models, and what are these models of?

In conventional usage the term "holy" is vague or mysterious because we have largely lost touch with any experience which it might reasonably describe. It has tended to become debased and signify mainly a facade of religiosity, an unspecified and bloodless make-believe virtue. Grotowski and Schechner offer a new definiton, which Grotowski calls "secular holiness", linked less to a conceptual than to a physical form.

For Grotowski, Schechner, and to a considerable extent, Peter Brook, "holiness" and "wholeness" signify a dimension of experience of intelligence and feeling beyond the limitations of normal activity. The individual performer and/or spectator feels 'complete' in the sense of being in command of and able to call upon an extended range of thought and action, less confined to the everyday level of perception, understanding and expression. Mind and body, left and right hemispheres of the brain, sensing and comprehending, work together instead of blocking each other, as frequently happens when the internal censor is on the job. However similar aims sought by Copeau, Lecoq and Keith Johnstone are not characterised to the same extent by terminology of religious derivation. This derivation as used by Grotowski is itself a hybrid. It originates in part in the Catholic ceremonial of Poland, and like comparable usage by e.g. Genet, is by no means unequivocal. Moreover, Grotowski, like Brook, also uses terms like "breaking down" and declares his goal to be a condition of "poverty" which appears to take up mediaeval Christian notions of "spiritual poverty", "renunciation" and asceticism, not to say mortification of the flesh as an abomination. (Philippe Gaulier describes Grotowski's approach as "de la flagellation" and is clearly very dubious about its benefits).

Additionally however Grotowski employs terms which appear to derive more from Eastern religious discourse such as "liberation" and "surrender", and it is of course well-known that Grotowski incorporated Indian performance training into his work after Eugenio Barba's return from the Kathakali Kalamandalam in South India – and that he subsequently downgraded the 'Eastern' framework under the impression that *yoga* tended to cultivate a kind of passivity. Grotowski's (and perhaps Barba's) grasp both of the derivation and the significance of the terms, as well as of the more profound workings of the practices, appears to be fairly superficial.

Some of Grotowski's terminology therefore suggests a firmly 'Western' Christian substratum and a largely dualistic framework: the "holy" can only emerge if the material/physical is subdued or sublimated. Eastern views by contrast are essentially monistic, they do not divide off mind and body, consciousness and matter; they also tend, with some exceptions, to emphasise joy and creativity as against suffering and renunciation. On the one hand then, we have attitudes and aims deriving from a reductionist/repressive model, on the other hand aspirations for organicity and openness: a juxtaposition of two entirely different understandings of reality and thus of the possibilities of human meaning.

Additionally we have a combination of religious terminology and a claim for the secular nature of the associated practice (though in fact Grotowski's demands on performers in his theatre, members of the audience and later, participants in his paratheatrical work, have frequently been described as similar to monastic discipline).

Is all of this indicative of fruitful interplay or confusion? It may quite likely include elements of both, and in this it resembles other transcultural acquisition. In order to get some sense of why this mixture should occur we need to consider the cultural context in which Grotowski's work arises. We need then to look at the aims of that work, both theatrical and para-theatrical, seen against that context; and to ask whether the effects and outcomes seem to bear out the intentions.

Grotowski's work appears to be located in an individualist and psychospiritual paradigm (nearer to Moreno than to Marx) in its demand for performers and audience to strip away the masks behind which we hide our vulnerability and existential isolation; in its early (theatrical) phase in particular it seeks also to transform that admission of individual anguish into a kind of shared suffering, a sort of transcendence through pain into *communitas*. Parallels with Polish experience in the 20th century have frequently been pointed out. But there seems to be little doubt that some of his performers and performances achieved an extraordinary intensity and luminosity.

Rooted in the Polish (Catholic, occupied, totalitarian) context the focus on both individual transcendence and communal suffering is comprehensible; in such conditions artists often feel themselves to be the last repository of the individual spirit, located precisely 'underground' (most Polish theatre taking place in cellars). A certain asceticism and self-sacrifice becomes the only way of preserving the individual creative spark. Schechner and Grotowski, like Peter Brook, also emphasise that the change in the configuration of self occurs in theatre through communion with others, as a public rather than private occasion. Theatre is both an individual and a social experience, with roots in common rituals which confirm, restore or revise the meanings we give to our lives for ourselves and for each other.

Somewhat fortuitously this politico-aesthetic, arising in its own quite specific context, happens to gel with the 1960s psychospiritual quest of disaffected capitalists, which has quite different causes but a not dissimilar perception of the situation of the individual under threat. During the same period (1960–1980, though with roots back as far as Artaud) theatre practitioners are themselves in quest of models for a "total" theatre which frequently also seeks to merge the spiritual and the physical, to demand "extra-daily" dynamics from performers and to seek to communicate this to receivers; in the course of which they collide with "New Age" psychology, psychotherapy and spiritual paradigms mainly derived from the East. Grotowski's paratheatrical work represents an ongoing dialogue with many of these factors; and is of course now located principally in the USA, and in an era conditioned by very different attitudes.

It is not surprising then that traces of all this are to be found in Grotowski. The historical and cultural factors outlined here clearly underlie that work, and the materialist or historicist argument they articulate is relevant. On the other hand, although in one sense this explains a lot, in another sense it explains nothing at all. We are no nearer understanding *how* performers in his theatre work acquired "presence", nor whether the training practices underlying those works and subsequently modified in the paratheatrical work are really significant factors in producing it. We are perhaps nearer to understanding why his explanations or formulations of what he believes himself to be doing are often paradoxical or confused. But we need to look at the practice in more detail.

Grotowski claims that his theatre, and the training methods he employs to produce it, bring about "liberation" from habitual forms of behaviour and definition of meaning. Before a theatre of wholeness can occur it must create actors who can perfect the attunement of their bodies to the transmission of the full range of spiritual, emotional, sensual and intellectual experience open to human beings. That means, as a prerequisite, the actor being able to suspend or put aside the concerns of the everyday personality. And to aim for that, as Grotowski and others do, is to regard the everyday personality level as caught up in restrictions, blocks, limited frameworks which throttle rather than permit full expression of human capacity. "The actor's accomplishment constitutes a transcendence of the half-measures of daily life" (Grotowski, *Towards a Poor Theatre*, 1975, 99). That in itself is a 'spiritual' view of human potential, equally found in psychological models: the necessary limitations of the reality principle can become internalised to such an extent that we shut off from all less immediate and less conscious needs and qualities, we strangle our own creative energy by confining it to the superficially materialistic exchange of the commonplace, leading in Freudian terms to explosions of frustration and despair.

Three further major concepts underlie Jerzy Grotowski's theatrical practice: "meeting" (Grotowski, 1975, 124), "disarmament" (1973, 121), and "holiday" (1973). Meeting involves a confrontation of actors with themselves and with the audience. It attempts a "disarming" or stripping away of the habitual pattern of reaction and response; its intention is – like that of Artaud – to produce a form of psychological liberation for performers, and by extension for participant-spectators (in many of Grotowski's productions a small and self-selecting group). The idea of holiday is used mainly in Grotowski's later, paratheatrical, period, though it has roots in his work in theatre production. The extension 'beyond' theatre derives in part from the experience that it is easier to train performers, with whom it is possible to work intensively, in a new way of experiencing themselves, than it is to do this for spectators. Hence Grotowski always required from his audience some evidence of their willingness to undergo a kind of initiation, reflected in the somewhat elitist composition of those who were prepared to enter into his 'difficult' theatrical experiments. This elitism is of course unsatisfactory in another sense, namely that it is exclusive; a feature which could be applied to the performances too, since the danger here is that highly-trained performers may use a code which looks from the outside very difficult to understand. Seen from another angle, "holiday" and "meeting" relativise the somewhat daunting severity of "disarmament" and suggest the possibility of play and mutual enjoyment as well as signalling the existence of a space-time enclosure in which the extra-daily can occur (and which might thus qualify as "performance" in Schechner's sense).

Both meeting and disarmament imply a removal of the protective clothing of habit; a readiness to explore and indeed become what is unfamiliar or scary. Perhaps it is scary, as Rilke suggests in *The Notebooks of Malte Laurids Brigge*, just because we have lost touch with it, and in meeting with it we meet with what is in a sense most ourself, but out of which we have constructed the very blocks which imprison us. Looking at this in physical terms, Grotowski uses exercises not simply to develop bodily skills, but rather to require the performer to pay close attention to the resistances or "obstacles" in the system. Exercises are often done slowly, as in *yoga*, with the aim of identifying the precise area of resistance and then working with it: it is the point at which you stop or draw back that is the mark of the physical and psychological border which needs to be extended. Meeting, as a training and performance strategy, thus requires a mixture of openness, vulnerability and spontaneity with a readiness for close and disciplined attention from all participants.

For the performers, the move towards the 'holy' condition occurs through what Schechner calls "subtraction" (1988, 179), as opposed to the "addition" of character acting. Disarmament is also referred to as "divestment", "self-sacrifice", "confession" (1975, 35ff., 207); and "surrender" (1973, 121). Grotowski claims the process leads towards "liberation" – like the Hindu *moksha*, going beyond attachment to the habitual dimensions of the everyday self. For Grotowski this *via negativa* produces a purification of the system, like a reduction of 'noise' in the machinery. Character acting gets the performer in touch with Stanislavsky's "emotional memory"; holy acting wants to probe an even more pre-conscious or pre-performative level, it attempts to 'wipe the performer clean' of existing configurations of feeling and behaviour, and to touch instead his or her tendencies to feeling and behaviour. The intention is something like Mallarmé's desire to return to the whiteness of the page between each word, which in effect means re-establishing contact with the state prior to all possible meanings. This readiness to move into action is the aim of much improvisation training, as used for instance by Keith Johnstone (*Impro,* 1981) and Jacques Lecoq. They demand a kind of anti-acting or non-acting first of all, in an attempt to help the performer to stop clinging on to an 'armour' of familiar moves and make these provisional instead of crystallised. (Johnstone's work has underpinned much actor development in Britain since the 60s, Lecoq's much of the best European physical theatre.)

Lecoq himself would probably reject any mystical overtones. By contrast, in Grotowski's case his written language has a heavily Catholic flavour, and his early repertoire has been called "theatre in extremis" (Hyde) – Artaudian aims physicalise the Mass, the Last Judgement, concentration camps, the Apocalypse. Given the history of Poland it is not surprising. The question is how far the rhetoric reflects a 'contamination' in the practice. Whereas Mallarmé's blank is essentially neutral in the sense that it does not imply any particular attitude or emotional tone, the note of "extremis" would suggest that Gaulier's description might not be too far off the mark. If "wipe clean" also implies a kind of sacrificial severity, this could well affect the outcome of the process. We are dealing here with refined or subtle experience: any trace of an affective mood will be extremely influential.

But what Grotowski is apparently seeking underneath or prior to these expressed forms is the process by which they come into being through body and consciousness. In workshops the instructions are likely to be neutral: you don't ask a performer to practise "sacrificing" him/herself, but you may say: 'Just do the exercise without trying for anything in particular.' Starting from the exploration of movements and resistances can, as for Lecoq, be an investigation of structures without necessary attachment to concepts, and it is moving towards something like a potential condition of language – verbal or physical. Coming at it from this end, instead of starting with the concept, means that you don't say 'be angry', but rather suggest a movement, a position, and explore what feelings it arouses, and then play with, vary, and develop them. On stage everything is articulated, significant. Yet it's also clear that underlying that enacted meaning is a resource level of skills and decisions which performers can employ. That can only happen fully if, for Grotowski, the habitual functioning, the safety-nets, of mind and body are somehow suspended or subdued: "the body must be freed from all resistance" (1975, 36). Any attempt at control from a superficial intellectual level must also be bypassed. This doesn't mean, I suspect, that the aim is a kind of soporific non-awareness. Rather, it seems to require an intensification of both discriminative and intuitive faculties, so that they can operate subtly, but are able to make adjustments discreetly and spontaneously. In other words, operate at a level of functioning where distinctions between mind and body, will and mechanics, scarcely exist. As for the virtuoso, the 'thought' of playing is also the 'act'.

Clive Barker (*Theatre Games*, 1977) calls this "body-think". Schechner suggests it is a state of high limbic arousal (1988, 278). Grotowski speaks of a "passive availability, which makes possible an active acting score" (1975, 37). For Lecoq, the performer in this condition is "disponible à l'évènement" ("open to what is happening"), with the imagination stimulated "à inventer des langages" ("to invent languages") (Lecoq, Brochure). The *via negativa* phase of surrender or disarmament leads into a situation where intelligent activity is ready and waiting, and can emerge without the hindrance of everyday taboos. Awareness is focussed through the body rather than separated from it by conceptualisation. Schechner suggests that a kind of observing self is in operation; something similar seems to happen in 'inner game' techniques used in sport, where an 'overdrive' condition is engaged. Nathalie Sarraute calls this "dédoublement" (*Entre la Vie et la Mort*, 1968) as applied to the business of writing: the alertness which can perceive words as they take shape from a feeling or image, and can temporarily suspend judgement; one part of the psyche is as it were observing the operation of another. The consciousness is involved on one level of functioning yet detached on another.

Here then it is clear on the one hand that Grotowski is on the track of something that may well be the "pre-expressive", and on the other hand that there is some danger of missing it: only fractionally, but in this zone fractions make all the difference. If the target of "availability" is hit, we are talking about the "pre-expressive" in the sense of awareness which is not involved with any object, which is as yet not focussed but simply in waiting, and we may also be talking about "presence" in the sense of alert readiness; if it is not, we are more likely talking about a form of "underscore", an emotional trace which will subtly determine whatever forms emerge.

Grotowski's "active score", Lecoq's "provocation to invent languages", do however suggest that the rhetorical and formulaic level of language may have been left behind. Grotowski's seriousness and Lecoq's playfulness look different, but they may be different paths to the same goal. Whether the method is through surrender or through play, which is itself often a form of surrender, a giving in or up to the moment, the result recalls Robbe-Grillet's claim that the business of art is to arrive at the point of playing with structure and thus liberating ourselves from the received modes which imprison thought, interaction, social organisation: "seules des organisations ludiques sont désormais possibles" ("henceforth only play structures are viable") (Robbe-Grillet, 1970). Grotowski thinks of performance as a discovery, which should "reach out into the unknown" and provide us with the "feeling of our own freedom" (1975, 97–98). Freedom is the ability to invent the score (and the under- or subscore) of our response to and articulation of experience.

Grotowski's third concept, "holiday", further emphasises the idea of play, and of the corporate and communal experience of theatre; it may be said to upstage Bahktin and link the carnivalesque with "research" into the processes of recreation and re-creation. Theatre takes place in 'time out' from everyday activity, and this liberation of time, place and functioning is what allows participants to begin to discover capacities everyday chronology squeezes out. (Holiday/holy day is also deliberately evoked here as another sign of the holistic intent; a further level of analysis based on distinctions made earlier would indicate that the 'sacred space' located here is precisely a space in consciousness/physiology: the 'space' or frame of consciousness and activity-in-waiting, as yet without trace of particular form.) Grotowski's later work in Poland (with his "University of Research" – see Kumiega), in California and in Italy takes the process beyond theatre into "meetings" of a more explicitly therapeutic nature. No public performance is envisaged, though the work still uses many drama-related exercises and is a preparation for any kind of performance. As Schechner also proposes, developing theatre-based skills is directly relevant to everyday operations, particularly since theatre is a highly appropriate model for the complex ways we acquire, process and communicate information. We learn in and through performance; and performing changes our relationship to our environment (we interact with it) and our understanding of that relationship. 'Holiday' also brings with it the sense of enjoyment; deriving from a sense of using more of one's capacities, it may function as a positive feed-back loop which makes subsequent performance more attractive. If it feels good, we want to go on doing it.

Attention to the 'whole body' in performance extends then from the body of the performer to that of the audience/co-participants. In his 'theatrical' period, Grotowski's productions of *Akropolis, Faust, The Constant Prince, Apocalypsis cum Figuris* not only make intense demands on the performers; they also by their use of the theatrical space and the disposition of the spectators in and around it force the latter to think about their relationship to the performance in new ways, as well as to confront their personal and national history through the interpretative slant of the production.

This shift of consciousness operates, both in the case of the audience and in that of the performers, as we have seen, through a *via negativa.* The spectators are disrupted, removed from comfortable roles both spatially (placed in odd locations in or under bits of set, for instance) and conceptually (made to experience themselves as judges or concentration camp victims). They are refused access to the kinds of habits a conventional audience might expect to indulge in. Romantic, Catholic and Communist heritage may all be presented as part of their physical situation vis-a-vis the performance, and these "sacred myths" (Grotowski, 1975, 43) are thus available to be relativised and deconstructed. By being asked to behave like this, the receivers are offered the chance to engage in 're(-)vision'; they also in a sense experience themselves as the 'theatre' in which the 'play' occurs, and as the source of much of the meaning of the process called 'text' (or texturing, or performance) which is occurring. Perhaps this could be thought of as a kind of "pre-receptivity". Like the availability of Grotowski's performers, it is only acquired through an experience of loss and defamiliarisation; but it may be argued that its outcome is to empower spectators rather than to use them as passive receptacles.

Grotowski's three concepts of meeting, disarmament and holiday all contribute to the idea of holiness or wholeness, subsequently employed in a similar sense by Schechner, Brook and others. Taken together they may balance each other: the masochistic overtones of a gloomy and savage dualism relativised by the holiday mood. In the light of this, holiness may be seen as a present imperfect rather than a future perfect, as a locating and playing with an improvisatory capacity. It implies reliance on internal rather than external sources, on physical immanence rather than any transcendental goal. Grotowski indicates that what you can't do is an important part of you: it is precisely the range of your ability to be different. Performance is always a risk because you offer the state you are in, with all its imperfections, to others; but the process of so doing can also be the means of suspending any familiar scoring and discovering possible new configurations.

Wholeness means incorporating everything. Holy theatre aims to return to the roots, to deconstruct the conventional concept of theatre by radicalising the experience of theatre. This radicalisation derives from a willingness to use anything suitable from among a wide range of methods of training and styles of performance, just as the idea of the holy involves bringing-together of disparate energies into a single focus. Theatre is here seen as a form of spiritual communion in which private and public experience meet and transform each other. For a member of the audience to move from spectator to participant changes his/her appreciation of the space and time of the environment ('theatre') and of the acts taking place within it; they are 'owned' in a more active sense. Thus both performers and spectators undergo a shift of role and activity.

In traditionally Catholic Poland, it is not surprising to find a religious subtext – more perhaps an overt text – to thinking about theatre. "The tendency to transform entertainment into ritual by means of theatre has been present in Grotowski almost from the beginning. His works have been played in churches, their themes are religious, the details of the performances are full of Polish Catholicism and Hassidic practices as well as materials drawn from Asian ritual traditions" (Schechner, 1988, 144). Nor is it surprising in a Catholic, Communist and post-Communist society that ritual and rhetoric are themselves viewed with suspicion but recognised as powerful factors in the creation of meaning. Witkiewicz and Kantor precede Grotowski; other groups such as Gardzienice and Theatre of the Eighth Day work with the same kind of programme but a more overtly political or social focus. Where Grotowski's work departs from the Polish context and engages with performance practice in the modernist/postmodernist transition phase is in the sometimes risky but potentially 'liberating' exploration of the holy as a site of change in performers, performances and receivers which operates across a sometimes confusing eclecticism of languages and practices. In the course of this exploration Grotowski offers a useful model for thinking about how we may rediscover the physicality of intelligence from which the reification of materialist thought has alienated us.

So Grotowski's work, seen in this light and in the context of developments in actor training and as a result in performance style, represents a shift in our conception of our own capabilities as performers; a dimension of human experience which might have been thought not to exist is rediscovered, found not to be merely a case of mystical aspiration but a physically available realilty. Holy theatre aims to restore the value of this moment, when nothing and everything come together.

References

Artaud, Antonin (1964) *Le Théâtre et son Double*. Paris: Gallimard

Barba, Eugenio (1979) *The Floating Islands*. Holstebrö: Thomsens

Barker, Clive (1977) *Theatre Games*. London: Methuen

Brook, Peter (1968) *The Empty Space*. London: Methuen

Frost, Anthony and Yarrow, Ralph (1990) *Improvisation in Drama*. London: Macmillan

Grotowski, Jerzy (1975) *Towards a Poor Theatre*. London: Methuen

Grotowski, Jerzy (1973) 'Holiday', *The Drama Review*, Vol. 17, no. 2

Hyde, George (1992) 'Polish Theatre', in *European Theatre 1960–1990*. Ed. Yarrow, Ralph. London: Routledge

Johnstone, Keith (1979) *Impro*. London: Methuen

Kumiega, Jennifer (1985) *The Theatre of Grotowski*. London: Methuen

Lecoq, Jacques Brochure for L'Ecole Jacques Lecoq, Paris

Maslow, Abraham (1968) *Towards a Psychology of Being*. New York: Van Nostrand Reinhold

Rilke, Rainer Maria (1988) *The Notebooks of Malte Laurids Brigge*. tr. S. Mitchell. London: Picador

Robbe-Grillet, Alain (1970) Article in *Le Nouvel Observateur*, (26/6/1970)

Sarraute, Nathalie (1968) *Entre la Vie et la Mort*. Paris: Gallimard

Schechner, Richard (1988) *Performance Theory*. London: Routledge

Contemporary Theatre Review
1997, Vol. 7, Part 1, pp. 35–47
Reprints available directly from the publisher
Photocopying permitted by license only

Barba's Concepts of the Pre-Expressive and the Third Organ of the Body of the Theatre and Theories of Consciousness

Daniel Meyer-Dinkgräfe

Theatre anthropology is the key concept in Barba's theatre theory and practice, and it subsumes a variety of concepts. Barba emphasises that the term "anthropology" is not used "in the sense of cultural anthropology" (Barba and Savarese, 1991, p. 8). Rather, theatre anthropology "is a new field of study applied to the human being in a performance situation" (*Ibid.*). Theatre anthropology incorporates both Occidental and Oriental theatre theory and practice and intends to provide "bits of advice" to the actor, rather than looking for universal principles or laws (*Ibid.*).

The actor is at the centre of theatre anthropology. Barba was inspired to set this priority by Grotowski and by his own interest in the actor's presence on stage:

> I am interested in a very elementary question: Why, when I see two actors doing the same thing, I get fascinated by one and not by the other. (Barba, 1985, p. 12)

Barba also uses the terms body-in-life or bios when analysing presence (Watson, 1993, p. 32). He distinguishes between daily behaviour, i.e. mainly unconscious "processes through which our bodies and voices absorb and reflect the culture in which we live" (*Ibid.*), and extra-daily behaviour, i.e. the specific codes of movement pertaining to specific performance forms, which, in their aesthetic function, differ from daily behaviour (cf. *Ibid.*).

Closely related to the concept of extra-daily behaviour is the concept of the pre-expressive, which Barba defines as:

> The level [of performance] which deals with how to render the actor's energy scenically alive, that is with how the actor can become a presence which immediately attracts the spectator's attention. (Barba and Savarese, 1991, p. 188)

Research has led Barba to differentiate three principles that govern the pre-expressive level of performance: "alterations in balance, the law of opposition, and (...) coherent incoherence" (Watson, 1993, p. 33). Whereas in daily behaviour, all movements of the body tend to follow the principle of least action, leading to a "minimum expenditure of energy for standing, sitting, and walking" (*Ibid.*), extra-daily behaviour of performance requires shifts in balance, which in turn lead to more energy being required for movement, for remaining still, or for retaining balance. The second principle, the law of opposition, is closely related to the alterations of balance. In both cases, daily behaviour patterns have to be distorted. In Western classical ballet the dancer maximises the opposition between body weight and gravity in "soaring feats of lightness and grace" (*Ibid.*, p. 34). The dancer spends much energy in the attempt to free himself/herself from the force of gravity.

The surplus of energy needed in performance is incoherent, it "makes no sense from a practical, daily life, point of view". However, it is also understandable, and in that sense coherent, that the actor spends this much more energy in extra-daily, performative activity, because the excessive energy expenditure is a major source of the dynamic in each of the performance genres (*Ibid.*, p. 35).

How can the performer radiate energy, establish "presence" and thus attract the spectator's attention? Barba argues that this is possible through a unity of three organs of the body of the theatre. The first organ is body technique, a physical mastery of extra-daily behaviour. The second is "the organ of u-topia", of "non-place", residing in the actor's viscera and his right hemisphere. "It is the super-ego which the presence of a master or masters has imbued us with during the transitions from daily technique to extra-daily performance technique" (Barba, 1988, p. 291). This organ transforms technique and raises it "to a social and spiritual dimension" (*Ibid.*). Barba describes the third organ as the "irrational and secret temperature which renders our actions incandescent" (*Ibid.*). Whereas the body and the "super-ego" can be trained, the elusive third organ is "our personal destiny. If we don't have it, no one can teach it to us" (*Ibid.*).

The pre-expressive as part of the body of the theatre is thus closely related to the performer's intuition (the u-topia), and to the third organ, which remains rather elusive, and which is the most explicit reference to consciousness among contemporary theatre theorists and artists. Nevertheless, the reference is vague and does not lead very far. As Watson points out,

> Barba is essentially a creative artist, a poet both in the theatre and in his writings about it. This poetic quality calls for a careful reading of his ideas since he favours poetic metaphors over the more traditional intellectual approach of deductive logic to sustain his arguments. (Watson, 1993, p. 18)

The relationship between mind and body, the phenomenon of the pre-expressive, and the three organs of the theatre's body have to be re-assessed from a cogent model of consciousness. Such a re-assessment will have to address the relationship between Western and Eastern training and performance techniques, traditions, and aesthetics, too, which are so central to Barba's intercultural theories.

The third organ is a state of consciousness beyond the intellect and beyond the emotions; it clearly represents a non-ordinary or altered state of consciousness. Traditionally, three major states of consciousness are distinguished: waking, dreaming, and sleeping. They are the "normal" states of consciousness. The term "normal" needs further explanation. What is "normal" is "defined by society and it is society's standards of perceptual normalcy that are part of an individual's personality" (Miletich, 1988, p. ix). Normal states of consciousness, then, are what society agrees to be the norm, the ordinary. Non-ordinary states of consciousness are referred to as "altered states of consciousness" (abbreviated ASC). In one of the first attempts to account for ASC, Ludwig describes general characteristics of ASC. They include alterations in thinking, a disturbed time sense, a loss of control, change in emotional experiences, a change of body images, perceptual distortions, changes in meaning or significance, a sense of the ineffable, a feeling of rejuvenation, and hypersuggestibility (cf. Ludwig, 1969, pp. 13–16). Ludwig also lists major ways of inducing ASC, and discusses the functions of ASC (cf. *Ibid.*, pp. 10–12). It is revealing that he supports seven maladaptive expressions by empirical evidence, but mentions only three adaptive expressions (healing, avenues of new knowledge and experience, social function) (cf. *Ibid.*, pp. 18–20). This emphasis on negative attributes of ASC is in line with Tart's claim that orthodox psychology regards ASC as "a temporary re-organisation of brain functioning", and Tart holds that "our ordinary state of consciousness is generally the most adaptive and rational way the mind can be organised, and virtually all ASCs are inferior or pathological", going into ASC spontaneously is a sign of mental illness, and "deliberately cultivating ASC is also a sign of psychopathology" (Tart, 1975, 60). This view, formulated in 1975, is supported by the choice of contents in an annotated bibliography on "States of Awareness" which lists articles on subjects such as depersonalisation, sleepwalking, amnesia, anaesthesia, thyroid disorders, near-death experience, *déja vu,* out of body experiences and sensory deprivation (Miletich, 1988), many of which would feature in psychopathology.

However, serious attempts can be found to account for and explain desirable and adaptive ASC. Clark constructs a map of mental states, similar to a map in geography. It "represents a large amount of information crowded into a very small space" (Clark, 1983, p. 1). He defines as "mind" "the whole range of mental states, i.e. of conscious states, sleeping and waking, which a person can experience" (*Ibid.*, p. 2). A "mental state" is defined as "the values taken by a person's set of "main" mental variables at any particular time" (*Ibid.*). The main variables are "mind work, general mood: pleasant or unpleasant; intensity of general mood and aspects of mind; online and off-line functions; sleeping or waking; concentration and diffusion of attention; and attention and things" (*Ibid.*, p. 13). Clark's incorporation of states of mental illness necessitate the inclusion of some extra variables such as "Anxiety; Obsessions; Compulsions; Phobias; Irritability; Hallucinations; Delusions; Pain; Disorientation; Anger; Fear; Guilt; Repugnance; Boredom; Depersonalisation; Derealization" (*Ibid.*, pp. 13–14). However, as opposed to other researchers writing about states of consciousness, Clark also incorporates desirable, "higher" mental states in his map. For this purpose, he discusses mysticism, which "concerns an unusual kind of experience obtained other than by the senses" (*Ibid.*, p. 16). Clark identifies seven main ideas in the content of mystical states, and relates those to some faculties of the mind (*Ibid.*, p. 20):

Seven main ideas (aspects of mind)		*Faculty*
K	Knowledge, significance	
U	Unity, belongingness	
E	Eternity, eternal now, being	Cognition
L	Light, exteroception	
B	Body sense, interoception	Perception
J	Joy	Emotion
F	Freedom	Volition

Clark also extracts certain recurrent comments on mystical states in the writings by the mystics. They are intensity; certainty; clarity; ineffability; sudden onset; and change of personality (cf. *Ibid.*). Finally, he differentiates between an average state, a state of peak experience (expressly borrowing the term from Maslow), and the mystical state proper (which is more intensive than the peak experience, but still within the range of being describable in words) (*Ibid.*, pp. 22–24). The climax of a transition from average state to peak experience to mystical experience proper is referred to as the "Void". Clark describes it as ineffable, and "a place of sudden transition" (*Ibid.*, p. 25), and associates it with the Buddhist concept of Nirvana. Another "set of members of the family of mystical states", termed "Dark" in quality, are also considered by Clark. They will not be of importance to the present study, however, and are therefore not further described here.

The attempt to provide consciousness with a basis is found in studies of the phenomenon of pure consciousness, the mystical state proper in Clark's terminology. The term "pure consciousness" is similar to the term used by Stace to describe the extraordinary state of consciousness reported by saints and sages throughout the ages: "pure unitary consciousness" (cf. Stace, 1960). Also in the context of mysticism, Forman edited a collection of essays explicitly dealing with "Pure Consciousness Events (PCE)", defined as "wakeful though contentless (non-intentional) consciousness" (Forman, 1990, p. 7). Placing the PCE within Stace's framework, Forman considers them as a form of what

W. T. Stace called "introvertive mysticism", which he distinguished from "extrovertive mysticism". In extrovertive mysticism one perceives a new relationship – one of unity, blessedness, reality (...) – between the external world and the self. In introvertive mysticism there is no awareness of the external world per se; the experience is of the Self itself. (*Ibid.*, p. 8)

Forman describes the current "received view" on all kinds of mystical experiences, including PCEs, as "constructivism" which argues that

mystical experience is significantly shaped and formed by the subject's beliefs, concepts and expectations. This view, in turn, emerged as a response to the so-called perennial philosophy school. Perennialists – notably William James, Evelyn Underhill, Joseph Maréchal, William Johnston, James Pratt, Mircea Eliade, and W. T. Stace – maintained that mystical experience represented an immediate, direct contact with a (variously defined) absolute principle. Only after that immediate contact with the "something more" according to this school, is such a direct contact interpreted according to the tradition's language and beliefs. (*Ibid.*, p. 3)

In the book, Forman assembles articles that argue in favour of the existence of PCEs, by looking at Yoga, Buddhist philosophy, the writings of Meister Eckhart, and Jewish mysticism. The articles in the second part of the book argue that "constructivism has not, and cannot plausibly account for these experiences" (*Ibid.*, p. 28).

Forman also provides a description of the experience of pure consciousness. It is from a subject just after instruction into the Transcendental Meditation technique:

I distinctly recall the first day of instruction [in the transcendental meditation technique], my first clear experience of transcending. Following the instruction of the teacher, without knowing what to expect, I began to drift down into deeper and deeper levels of relaxation, as if I were sinking into my chair. Then, for some time, perhaps for a minute or a few minutes, I experienced a silent inner state of no thoughts; just pure awareness and nothing else; then again I became aware of my surroundings. It left me with a sense of deep ease, inner renewal, and happiness. (Alexander, unpub.)

Forman comments: "It is striking that the subject notes that he did not "know what to expect", for this tends to support the claim that one may have a PCE even without the purportedly shaping expectations" (Forman, 1990, p. 27).

The third organ as intuited by Barba is likely to be pure consciousness. Barba argued that it is either available or not, that it cannot be trained. This claim has to be carefully considered.

In the development of theatre theory and practice from Diderot to Barba, the body's role in acting and actor training has received increasing attention. This development is proportional to at least four factors: first, to the increase in scientific knowledge of physiological processes. The second reason for increasing interest in the body's role in performance is the growing disillusionment with numerous psychological theories which failed to provide a consensus either regarding the structure and functioning of the human psyche or the relationship of mind and body. The third reason is the growing interest in Indian dance forms which were interpreted as using and affecting mainly the body. Finally, the concept of disponibilité, developed by Jacques Lecoq, has to be taken into account in the context of the body-orientated performance art of improvisation.

Assessing the insights yielded by an increase in scientific knowledge of physiological processes, Pradier develops a biological theory of the body in performance. Some of the issues he addresses are:

(a) the epiphanic system, defined as

> (...) the sum of physical (visual, acoustic, tactile) and physico-chemical constants pertaining to the performer that can act consciously or unconsciously on a receiver, either directly or indirectly, separately or combined. (Pradier, 1990, p. 88)

(b) Performance activity illustrating the holistic aspect of human behaviour:

> the most elaborate types of behaviour always include a component of sensory and motor responses (i.e. body memory, movements involved with language activity, etc). The physiological processes of stabilisation, development, and preservation of the integrity of the central nervous system (CNS) always include a performing aspect. (*Ibid.*, pp. 88–89)

(c) Pradier proposes that the performing arts "correspond to an instinctive magnification of biological motions" (*Ibid.*, p. 89). The concept of biological motion is related to an experiment:

> When a small number of lights are placed on the limbs and joints of a moving human – or animal – the motions of the lights dubbed "biological motions" (...) are sufficient to enable adult observers to perceive immediately the activity of the human. (*Ibid.*)

(d) Research suggests that performance "acts on the immune system of the performers" (*Ibid.*, p. 91). Pradier concludes that it must, in consequence, also affect the audience's immune system. In support of this hypothesis, Pradier refers to a controversial experiment carried out at Harvard University: saliva taken from spectators watching a film of Mother Theresa's healing activities in Calcutta showed a higher rate of antibodies which protect against respiratory infections (IgA) (cf. *Ibid.*, p. 92).

(e) The psychic exaltation of the actor, no matter whether professional or not, associated with an increase of neuro-hormones (which has yet to be verified empirically), makes it tempting for Pradier to see "a performance as a kind of neuro-hormonal reward auto-stimulation" (*Ibid.*).

(f) The performing arts, especially its elements of dance and mime, "have a sensory-motor stimulation function for the audience" (*Ibid.*, p. 93). In this context, Pradier uses the term "restoration", and he expressly puts it into the context of Schechner's use of that term: Pradier wants to

> signal a "biological restoration" as opposed to the "biological decadence" observed in daily life among most cultures. By visually and auditorily working on movement and acoustic patterns, actors/dancers/singers can help the audience have a stronger and more holistic and balanced alignment, a kind of embodiment. (*Ibid.*, p. 94)

(g) Pradier presents a comprehensive list of open issues regarding possible connections of performance and biological rhythms, e.g. "Are rhythms in the performing arts also based on a neural time code (...)?" (*Ibid.*).

Regarding Lecoq's concept of disponibilité, Frost and Yarrow define improvisation as

> the skill of using bodies, space, all human resources, to generate a coherent physical expression of an idea, a situation, a character (even, perhaps, a text); to do this spontaneously, in response to the immediate stimuli of one's environment, and to do it (...) as though taken by surprise, without preconceptions. (Frost and Yarrow, 1990, p. 1)

Disponibilité, as defined by Lecoq, is not just a theory but an experiential condition; a way of being which can be sought and found. It sums up

> in a single term the condition improvisers aspire to: it offers a way of describing an almost intangible and nearly undefinable state of being: having at (or in) one's fingertips, and any other part of the body, the capacity to do and say what is appropriate, and to have the confidence to make the choice. Its a kind of total awareness, a sense of being at one with the context, script, if such there be, actors, audience, theatre space, oneself and one's body. (*Ibid.*, p. 152)

Disponibilité is thus characterised by an experience of total presence in the present, from moment to moment. Since the body can be experienced, and such experience described in words more tangibly than an (altered state of) consciousness, and because the theories of ASC are vague and contradictory, it is no wonder that discourse in performance (theory and practice) concentrates on the body rather than the mind, and that Barba's statements about the third organ remain vague.

A very interesting model of the mind, of consciousness, a model which also incorporates the mind-body relationship, has been proposed in recent years by Maharishi Mahesh Yogi. He is a disciple of the late Swami Brahmananda Saraswati (1869–1953), who held the position of Shankaracharya of Jyotir Math for the last 13 years of his life. This is one of four monasteries in India founded by the sage and philosopher Shankara to safeguard the tradition of his Advaita Vedanta philosophy. Brahmananda Saraswati has been called "Vedanta incarnate" by India's first President, Radhakrishnan (Campbell, 1975). As Brahmananda Saraswati's disciple, Maharishi Mahesh Yogi is in the direct line of Shankara's Advaita Vedanta Philosophy. Maharishi Mahesh Yogi has subjected traditional assumptions of Indian philosophy to a rigorous reassessment, termed Vedic Science. Within this field, Vedic Psychology is of particular importance to this study.

The theory and practice of Vedic Psychology maintains that the human nervous system enables the direct experience of pure consciousness. In asserting this possibility, Vedic Psychology is in line with the mystics and those who, like Forman, accept their experiences as real and natural. Unlike the mystics, Vedic Psychology holds that through mental techniques which can be learnt easily, everyone can have this experience, not only a few isolated individuals.

Pure consciousness as described by Vedic Psychology resembles the description of "pure unitary consciousness", a term coined by Stace in his survey of mysticsim. Gelderloos and Beto argue that the characteristics of pure consciousness as defined by Vedic Psychology are similar to the characteristics of "pure unitary consciousness" as described by Stace (Gelderloos and Beto, 1989). The following aspects are shown to be similar: ego quality, unifying quality, inner subjective quality, temporal/spatial quality, noetic quality, ineffability, positive affect, and religious quality.

Vedic Psychology proposes pure consciousness as the basis of more expressed levels of awareness, and a hierarchical structure of the mind, defined as the "overall multilevel functioning of consciousness" (Alexander, 1990, p. 290). On levels characterised by increasing concreteness, activity, diversity, and decreasing subtlety, the field of pure consciousness gives rise to the individual ego, the level of feelings, emotion and intuition, the intellect, the mind, the desires, and the senses. This sequence of structures of the mind corresponds to traditional Vedic literature, particularly *samkhya* and *yoga* (Sinha, 1979), where ahamkara (ego), buddhi (intellect), manas (mind), akasha (space, the object of the sense of hearing), vayu (air, the object of the tactile sense), tejas (fire, the object of the sense of sight), apas (water, the object of the sense of taste), and prithivi (earth, the object of the sense of smell) are differentiated (Alexander, 1990, p. 290). In addition, Vedic Psychology locates emotion, feeling and intuition between the levels of ego (ahamkara) and intellect (buddhi).

In principle, each subtler level can "observe and monitor the more expressed levels" (Alexander, 1990, p. 290), with the level of pure consciousness, being at the basis of all expressions of the mind, informing all levels of the mind. This principle is in line with Bohm's theory of the relationship between mind and matter when he claims that thoughts can be regarded as a series of

> more and more closely woven nets. Each can "catch" a certain context of corresponding "fineness". The finer nets cannot only show up the details of form and structure of what is "caught" in the coarser nets; they can also hold within them a further context that is implied in the latter. (Bohm, 1990, p. 282.)

In Vedic Psychology, the ego is further defined as the inner value of the experiencer, the most immediate expression of the field of pure consciousness. The concept of ego is thus different from those of Freud, Jung or other Western psychologists.

The emotions, feelings and intuition are closely related to the ego. The intellect, again both cosmic and individual, is characterised by its discriminating abilities, and it is this quality of discrimination that the intellect takes up from the field of pure consciousness, which "is capable of discriminating both knower and known" within its own self-referral structure (Alexander, 1990, p. 290). It should be noted that the term "mind" in Vedic Psychology refers both to "the whole range of mental activity and structure, in contrast to pure consciousness on the one hand or the body on the other" (*Ibid.*) and to "the specific level of thinking within that overall structure" (*Ibid.*). The function of the mind on the individual level, is to consider possibilities and their relationships, and it "also serves the functions of memory and thought" (Dillbeck, 1988, p. 264). Desire also originates in a particular characteristic of the field of pure consciousness, its desire to know itself. It connects the mind and the senses with the environment: "Desire may be understood as motivating the flow of attention and thus, in daily experience, connecting the mind with the environment through the senses" (*Ibid.*).

Vedic Psychology does not stop at describing the interrelationship of the elements of consciousness and pure consciousness as their source. In answer to the question "What are the highest possible forms of human development?" (Alexander, 1990, p. 3), Vedic Psychology proposes that it is possible not only to have occasional experiences of higher states of consciousness as described by the mystics, or called "peak experiences" by Maslow, but to systematically develop such more advanced states of consciousness as phenomena of permanent daily experience.

The exploration of adulthood has only recently attracted "significant attention from developmental psychologists" (*Ibid.*). Focal point of the emerging theories is the relationship of proposed models of higher stages of human development to the seminal theory of cognitive development advanced by Jean Piaget. He differentiated distinct developmental stages, leading to an endpoint termed "formal operations":

> For him [Piaget], formal operations is the culmination of cognitive development: there is no further development of the organisational form of thought beyond this stage; remaining changes are in terms of increased competence with formal operations and their more comprehensive application in the accumulation of greater knowledge. (*Ibid.*, p. 5)

The developmental stage of formal operations is normally attained, according to Piaget, during the teen years. It thus belongs to "preadult development, even though full facility in this mode of thinking may not develop until adulthood – or may never develop" (*Ibid.*).

Alexander holds that assessing the possibilities of adult development beyond Piaget's stage of formal operations, involves three related issues:

> Does development towards the endpoint proceed through qualitatively distinct stages? What mechanisms underlie this development? What major areas get developed (e.g., cognition and affect), and how do they interrelate? (*Ibid.*, p. 3)

Alexander differentiates non-hierarchical and hierarchical theories, theories of advanced moral development, and theories of consciousness and self-development (cf. *Ibid.*, pp. 9–10). The concepts of adult development proposed by Vedic Psychology fall into the last category.

Based on the proposition to regard pure consciousness as a fourth state of consciousness next to the commonly known and experienced ones – waking, dreaming, and sleeping – Vedic Psychology describes three further stages of consciousness development. Termed "cosmic consciousness", a fifth state of consciousness is characterised by the coexistence of waking, or dreaming, or sleeping, and pure consciousness. In cosmic consciousness, the level of pure consciousness, which is never overshadowed in daily experience by the activities and experiences of the individual psyche, becomes a "stable internal frame of reference from which changing phases of sleep, dreaming, and waking life are silently witnessed or observed" (Alexander, 1989, p. 342). Just as the states of waking, dreaming, sleeping, and of pure consciousness can be researched with reference to different, and state-specific subjective experiences as well as equally different and state-specific patterns of bodily functions such as EEG activity, eye movement, metabolic rate, breathing patterns, Galvanic skin response, and concentrations of various hormones in the blood, which are open to psychophysiological empirical studies, cosmic consciousness, too, has its state-specific patterns of subjective experience and psychophysiological variables. The *Bhagavad-Gita*, an important part of the *Mahabharata*, describes the experience of an individual who has gained the state of cosmic consciousness like this: "He who sees that all work, everywhere, is only the work of nature; and that the spirit watches his work – he sees the truth" (Mascaro, 1962, p. 101).

The following is a description of witnessing dreaming:

> Often during dreaming I am awake inside, in a very peaceful, blissful state. Dreams come and go, thoughts about the dreams come and go, but I remain in a deeply peaceful state, completely separate from the dreams and the thoughts. My body is asleep and inert, breathing goes on regularly and mechanically, and inside I am just aware that I am. (Alexander, 1989, p. 348)

This doubleness of experience, pure consciousness witnessing the activities of waking, dreaming, and sleeping, is not equivalent to an uncomfortable dissociation or spilt personality.

The next stage of development, according to Vedic Psychology, is called "refined cosmic consciousness". In cosmic consciousness, the field of pure consciousness is permanently experienced together with waking, or dreaming, or sleeping. This level of functioning is maintained in refined cosmic consciousness and "combined with the maximum value of perception of the environment. Perception and feeling reach their most sublime level" (*Ibid.*).

The British poet Kathleen Raine reports her experience of seeing a hyacinth, suggestive of an experience of refined cosmic consciousness as predicted by Vedic Psychology:

> I dared scarcely to breathe, held in a kind of fine attention in which I could sense the very flow of life in the cells. I was not perceiving the flower but living it. I was aware of the life of the plant as a slow flow or circulation or a vital current of liquid light of the utmost purity. I could apprehend as a simple essence formal structure and dynamic process. This dynamic form was, as it seemed, of a spiritual not a material order; or of a finer matter, or of matter itself perceived as spirit. There was nothing emotional about this experience which was, on the contrary, an almost mathematical apprehension of a complex and organised whole, apprehended as whole, this whole was living; and as such inspired by a sense of immaculate holiness. (...) By "living" I do not mean that which distinguishes animal from plant or plant from mineral, but rather a quality possessed by all these in their different degrees. (Raine, 1975, p. 119)

The final level of human development according to Vedic Psychology is called "unity consciousness". In this state of consciousness, "the highest value of self-referral is experienced" (Alexander, 1989, p. 359). The field of pure consciousness is directly perceived as located at every point in creation, and thus "every point in creation is raised to the (...) status" of pure consciousness (*Ibid.*). "The gap between the relative and absolute aspects of life (...) is fully eliminated" (*Ibid.*, p. 360). The experiencer experiences himself and his entire environment in terms of his own nature, which he experiences to be pure consciousness. The *Bhagavad-Gita* describes unity consciousness thus:

> He whose self is established in
> Yoga, whose vision everywhere is
> even, sees the Self in all beings
> and all beings in the Self.
> (Maharishi Mahesh Yogi, 1969, p. 359)

How can the conceptualisation of consciousness offered by Vedic Psychology help to understand Barba's elusive third organ in his notion of the body of the theatre, in relation to the other two organs? The basis of all of the performer's activities on the stage depends, in Barba's view, on whether or not the performer has got the third organ. The third organ has been identified as the field of pure consciousness. According to Vedic Psychology, it is a field that is at the basis of every individual consciousness. It is only a question whether this level of consciousness is open to awareness, or whether (and to what extent) it is overshadowed by sensory impressions. The first and second organ in Barba's concept of the body of the theatre are located on manifest levels of pure consciousness: the second organ, representing the innate principles of extra-daily behaviour, is structured on the level of intuition, whereas the first organ, i.e. the actual body techniques of extra-daily behaviour, is even more manifest or expressed, reaching beyond the senses into the physical body.

Assessing Barba's theories from the perspective of Vedic Psychology not only provides a cogent framework of understanding. It also allows a modification of Barba's argument to the extent that training of the third organ is possible, after all: it is possible to develop human consciousness. In the course of that development, experience of pure consciousness increases, to be ultimately co-existent with waking, or dreaming, or sleeping (cosmic consciousness). Throughout the further development to refined cosmic consciousness and unity consciousness, the permanent experience of pure consciousness is maintained. The insight that the apparently most elusive level of the art of the performer can be understood, theorised, experienced and developed, might well prove the beginning of a rewarding new chapter of theatre research.

References

Alexander, Charles N., and Robert W. Boyer (1989) "Seven States of Consciousness: Unfolding the Full Potential of the Cosmic Psyche in Individual Life through Maharishi's Vedic Psychology", *Modern Science and Vedic Science* 2:4, pp. 324–371

Alexander Charles N. *et al.* (1990) "Growth of Higher Stages of Consciousness: Maharishi's Vedic Psychology of Human Development", in Charles N. Alexander and Ellen J. Langer, eds., *Higher Stages of Human Development. Perspectives on Human Growth* (New York, Oxford: Oxford University Press)

Alexander, Charles N. and Ken Chandler, Robert W. Boyer (1990) "Experience and Understanding of Pure Consciousness in Vedic Science of Maharishi Mahesh Yogi", unpublished paper, 5–6, quoted in Forman, pp. 27–28

Barba, Eugenio (1985) "Interview with Gautam Dasgupta", *Performing Arts Journal*

Barba, Eugenio (1988) "The Way of Refusal: the Theatre's Body-in-Life", *NTO*, 4:16, pp. 291–299

Barba, Eugenio, and Nicola Savarese (1991) *The Secret Art of the Performer. A Dictionary of Theatre Anthropology.* (London, New York: Routledge)

Bohm, David (1990) "A new theory of the relationship between mind and matter" *Philosophical Psychology* 3:2, pp. 121–138

Campbell, Anthony (1975) *The Mechanics of Enlightenment. An Examination of the Teaching of Maharishi Mahesh Yogi* (London: Gollancz)

Clark, John H. (1983) *A Map of Mental States* (London, Boston, Melbourne and Henley: Routledge and Kegan Paul)

Dillbeck, Michael C. (1988) "The Self-Interacting Dynamics of Consciousness as the source of the Creative Process in Nature and in Human Life " *Modern Science and Vedic Science* 2:3, pp. 245–278

Forman, Robert K. C. (1990) "Introduction: Mysticism, Constructivism, and Forgetting", in Robert K. C. Forman ed., *The Problem of Pure Consciousness. Mysticism and Philosophy* (New York, Oxford: Oxford University Press)

Frost, Anthony and Ralph Yarrow (1990) *Improvisation in Drama.* New Directions in Theatre (London: Macmillan)

Gelderloos, Paul, and Zaid H. A. D. Beto (1989) "The TM- and TM-Sidhi Program and Reported Experiences of Transcendental Consciousness", *Psychologia* 32:2, pp. 91–103

Ludwig, Arnold M. (1969) "Altered States of Consciousness", in Charles T. Tart, ed., *Altered States of Consciousness. A Book of Readings* (New York, London, Sydney, Toronto: John Wiley and Sons)

Maharishi Mahesh Yogi (1969) *On The Bhagavad-Gita. A New Translation and Commentary, chapters* 1–6 (Harmondsworth: Penguin).

Mascaro, Juan, (transl). (1962) *The Bhagavad-Gita* (Harmondsworth: Penguin Books)

Miletich, John J. (1988) *States of Awareness. An Annotated Bibliography* (New York, Westport, London: Greenwood)

Pradier, Jean-Marie (1990) "Towards a Biological Theory of Performance", NTQ VI: 21, pp. 86–98

Raine, Kathleen (1975) *The Land Unknown* (NewYork: George Braziller)

Sinha, Nandalal (transl.) (1979) *The Samkhya Philosophy* (New Delhi: Oriental Books Reprint Company)

Stace, W. T. (1960) *Mysticism and Philosophy* (London: Macmillan)

Tart, Charles T. (1975) "Some assumptions of orthodox Western psychology", in Charles Tart, ed., *Transpersonal Psychologies* (London: Routledge and Kegan Paul), pp. 59–111

Watson, Ian (1993) *Towards a Third Theatre. Eugenio Barba and the Odin Teatret* (London and New York: Routledge)

Contemporary Theatre Review
1997, Vol. 7, Part 1, pp. 49–57
Reprints available directly from the publisher
Photocopying permitted by license only

Pre-Expressivity: Some Thoughts from the Rehearsal Floor

John Martin

What springs to mind with this phrase, "pre-expressivity"? A kaleidoscope of images and sensations: the awe I feel working with many performers from non-western cultural traditions who seem to have their energy at their finger-tips drawing our attention to them; the desire to instil in my performers and my students that control of energy which brings all their physical, vocal and improvisational training together as a latent force with which they can create, express, perform.

And of course I think of Eugenio Barba talking, talking, talking about the dynamics he has extracted from the invited performers on his laboratory table. He formulates beautifully these elements which will make up the pre-expressive performer, but I always have an uncomfortable feeling that he finds what he went looking for, not what was really there. And although he has been observing all this for years and years he refuses to, or is incapable of, formulating a training to pass on this knowledge. He leaves it all hanging in the void, not absorbed or integrated even into his own actors.

Long before meeting Eugenio I had wondered at the "presence" of the Kathakali actor in preparation, before he takes on the character, before he approaches the audience and wished my actors had some of that quality.

And frequently, after meeting him, I observed, in my work, theatrical states like the amazingly focussed concentration of the Noh Theatre actor in training (just as earlier I had trained to attain the "ready" body of the classical ballet dancer), and although realising it is the result of years of terrifyingly hard training, I was able to see certain elements of control which I could pass on, in practical training exercises, to my actor colleagues.

And then this called up part of my own basic training in one of the European Theatre's realisations of the need for the actor to have a level of presence in the body before tackling character. This was the study of the neutral mask, in my case taught by Jacques Lecoq. Neutrality, in this work, is a state of alertness, readiness in the actor, not in the character, poised for expression.

So with all these elements in my background, how do I use this information as a director, or as a trainer of actors?

With a background of physical theatre and a profound interest in, and admiration for, theatre forms of other cultures, I have been mind-numbingly bored by so much British theatre. When I take Peking Opera actors to London theatre, they cannot understand why the actors on stage behave "with no eyes and no body", in other words with no more energy than people on the street. I have to agree, and I cannot count the times I have fallen asleep in the theatre or walked out in breast-tightened frustration because the actors are so tedious.

Of course there are exceptions, actors who have that focus of attention and readiness which we seek in pre-expressiveness, but what are they? There are the actors who are "naturally talented", who seem to pull your attention as they enter stage, but did they train for this or is it some strange permutation of physical and mental attributes they have inherited genetically or developed unwittingly?

Then there are the "dangerous" actors. When they are on stage there is something wild about them which is, in an exciting way, unsettling. We have no idea what they might do – they are unpredictable. (Compare Zhou Shao Lin's statement "The good actor goes on stage setting up a rhythm, as soon as the audience feels the rhythm he must break it, surprise them, never let them know how the rhythm will continue. That will keep their attention".)

Peter O'Toole is a great example of the dangerous actor. Even in the most abysmal of plays, and even when his character is poorly written he, the actor, is dangerous and exciting. It is not just the glint in his eye (the actor's eye, not the character's), it is the taut, steely body like a cat about to spring, in any direction. Phillipe Gaulier also strives for this danger of the unexpected in his teaching, urging his students not to do what they know they can do well, what is safe, but he teaches through a route of highly destructive sarcasm and negativity which can also destroy creativity.

But I cannot teach "natural" talent or "danger" (apart from encouraging risk taking). I have to look for something else to make performers energised and therefore more interesting and fascinating, yes, "magical" than they are. Without a doubt I need them to have some state before they go on stage, even before they go into the work, a physical state, a mental state, a combination of these.

I remain totally unconvinced that Barba has succeeded in finding a route and seems stuck in an impasse of his own making, but some of his analysis is fascinating and can lead to further enquiry which will give a more fulfilling knowledge when working with performers from India, China, Japan, West Africa, Indonesia, and many other cultures.

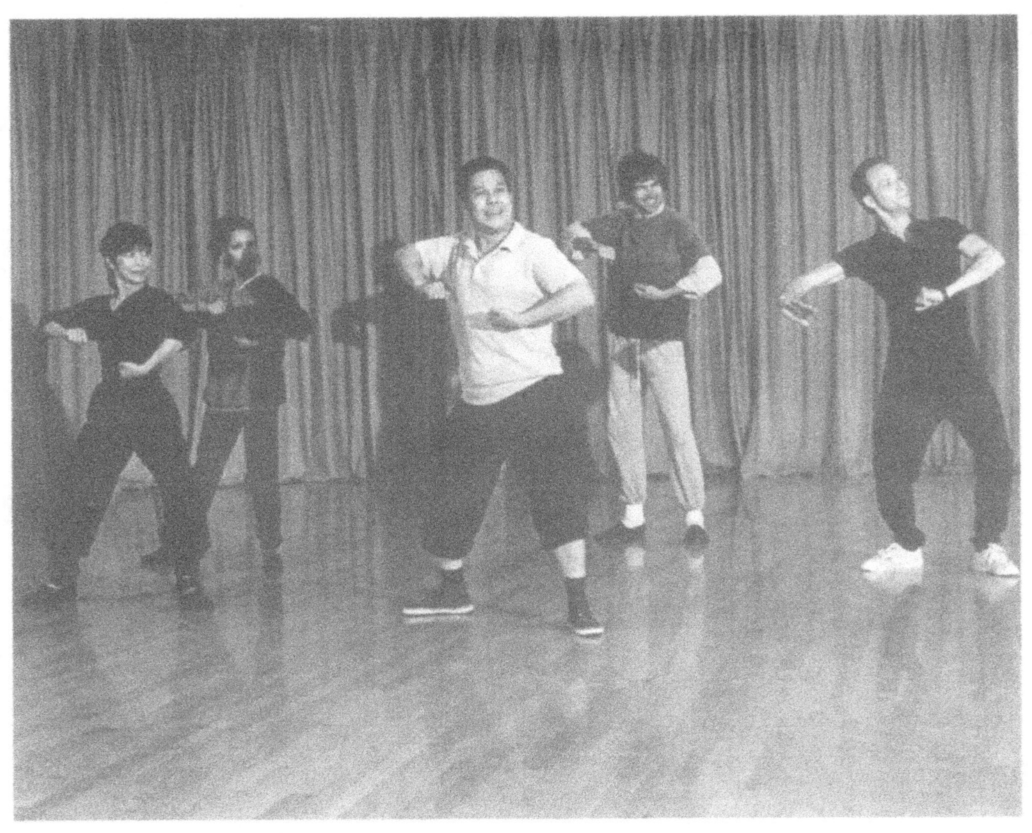

1. Ma Ming Qun leads a Peking Opera class for Pan Project's Intercultural Summer School. Photo: Graham de Smidt

From such research I can teach specific exercises of breathing from Noh, of spinal and abdominal control from Kabuki, of physical base from Yoruba dance drama, or rhythmic precision from South India, just as I can teach the dynamics of mime via Decroux or Lecoq. I see the actors flourish, I see them take control of the space around them, I see them commanding their own work. But is this truly pre-expressive? Only partly so because these actors seldom reach that immensity of power in the Noh or Kathakali actor, nor even the quiet magnetic control of an actor like Yoshi Oida in Brook's production of "The Man Who" where, in spite of my grave misgivings about the play, I found his every look or gesture showed a fantastic focusing of his and our attention.

And I am also aware that the teaching of these concepts to Western actors, as well as taking an enormous amount of time, and being from traditions which conserve their forms rather than evolve them, is often part of a psychology of theatre which I have found to be anti-creative. This involves an authoritarian forcing the actor into a technique, or even (and the word is used) "breaking" the actor down in order to rebuild him or her.

This is a surprisingly common theme in western experimental theatre, which tries to purge the performers of their existing styles, idiosyncrasies etc., rendering them "neutral" in the most negative way.

Done caringly this is a possible way of forming new performers. It does not, however, work so well with experienced performers who have already developed their techniques, and their methods of channelling their energies. Moreover it is often carried out with a psychological brutality which can leave the performer frustrated, not understanding and with no confidence.

I have experienced (I want to say suffered) this from Grotowski and from Lecoq and have heard of it about other reputable names.

So if we are not to follow this path, what could be a way of giving a western performer the state of pre-expressiveness which I frequently need in my actors?

I can take them through the neutral mask in a positive and caring way; caringly I can lead them to discover held strength from a number of training disciplines from non-western theatre styles. But then, what is the "gelling" agent? What in the western performer can elevate them to the desired state?

Twice I have found answers, from two different sources, which I have been able to develop into games and exercises.

The first was in reading the autobiography of Jean-Louis Barrault. In it he describes the type of actors whom he finds bring life to his work. He wants actors who are like kittens, who can play with a total and undivided concentration, being inventive with a ball of wool, joyous as they leap, scowl, bite, roll, attack; and then can break completely and wander off, carrying no "baggage" from it, to find something new.

This made sense to me immediately. This state of alert playfulness is a state which actors in the west can understand, whether with the alertness of a cat or of a sportsman. It makes them ready and creative, unpredictable but co-operative. And if this playfulness is mixed with some of the energy disciplines alluded to above there is an excitement, a pre-expressive playfulness which aids both the creative process of rehearsal and the joy of performance. This readiness in action for the themes of character, situation or emotion can be injected through this state of play.

Joy! This was my second key. It came from talking to and working with Indian performer Mallika Sarabhai, who had been through an experience of working with a European director in which some of the above-mentioned techniques of "breaking down" had been used. She had been asked to forget that she was a dancer, and that she was Indian, two of the things which most strongly identify her.

Although she had learned much from the overall experience, she had considerable resentment at this method and contrasted it strongly with her Indian experience of creativity which had always been in a spirit of "*anand*" – joy.

Again this linked immediately with so many remarks that performers around the world had made and provided the counterpoint to the rather gruelling methods I have seen too often and which leave actors drained and energy-less.

Joy might be a strange concept to the Western mind, and conjure up something all too flippant, unserious (even hippy-ish), but it is not far from the idea of play, and relies on the idea that art must be enjoyable, uplifting, even when dealing with serious subjects. If there is no joy in creating how can the performance be enjoyable for the audience?

Sarabhai speaks of *anand* as something which is not taught in any formal sense, but absorbed as an atmosphere of work both by being with those who have already absorbed it (in the traditional guru–shishya relationship) and by a build-up of elements which make the work "special", extra-daily. She speaks with despair and an inability to understand the average European performer's behaviour in rehearsal and in preparation for performance. To her it is banal, dragging in the minutiae of the quotidian, when what is needed is a lifting out of the everyday into that special place of creativity. To the Indian performer there is a small ritual of entering the rehearsal/performance space, shoes would never be worn there, the teacher's feet will be touched, the musicians and instrument will be "saluted", and often the performer will have a small ritualised set of movements to lift him/her into a state of readiness. Whereas these micro-rituals might put the average European performer into a rather serious state of self-importance (perhaps reflecting Christian ritual), the same elements rid Indian performers of

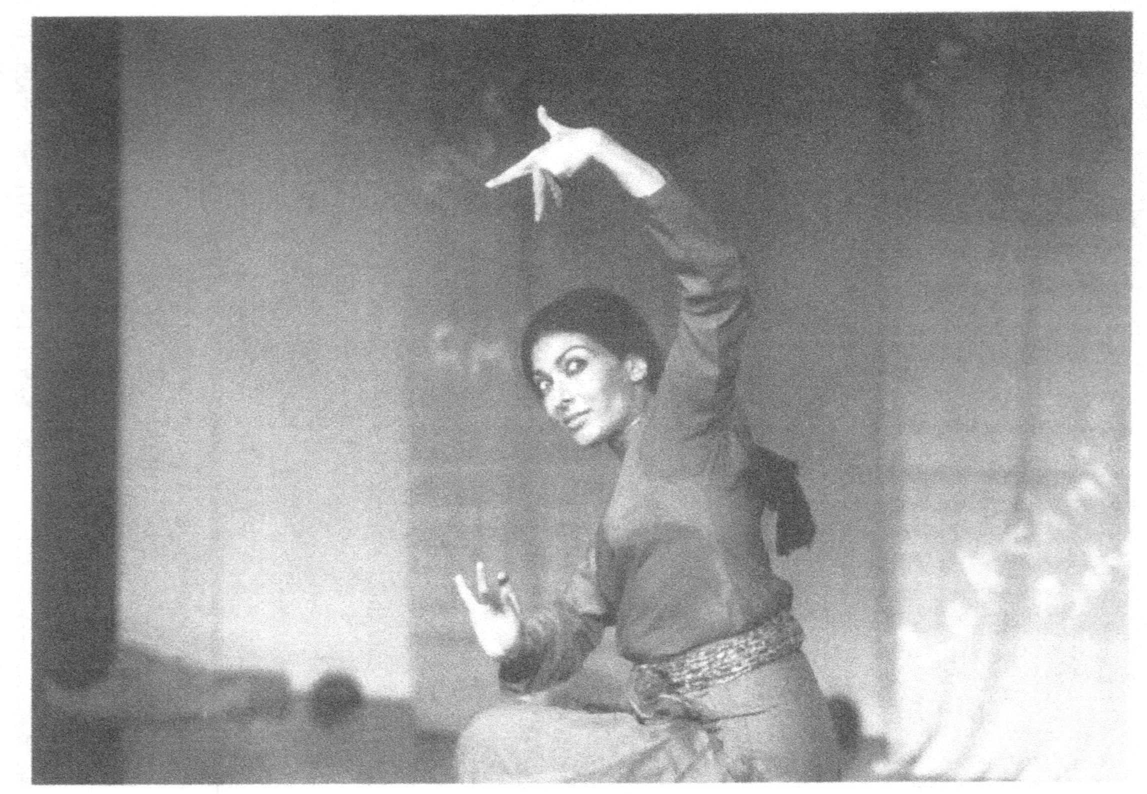

2. Mallika Sarabhai in John Martin's production of *Shakti – The Power of Women*. Photo copyright Gilles Abegg

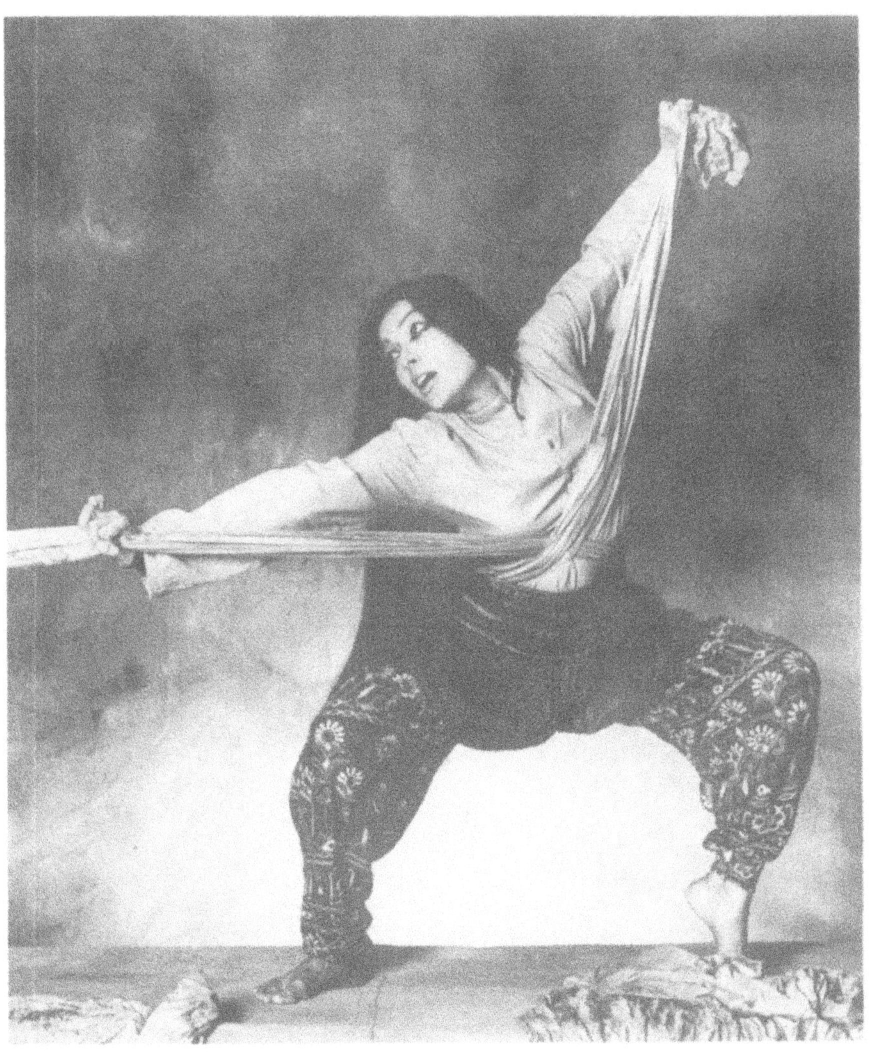

3. Mallika Sarabhai in John Martin's production of *Shakti – The Power of Women*. Photo: Eric Richmond

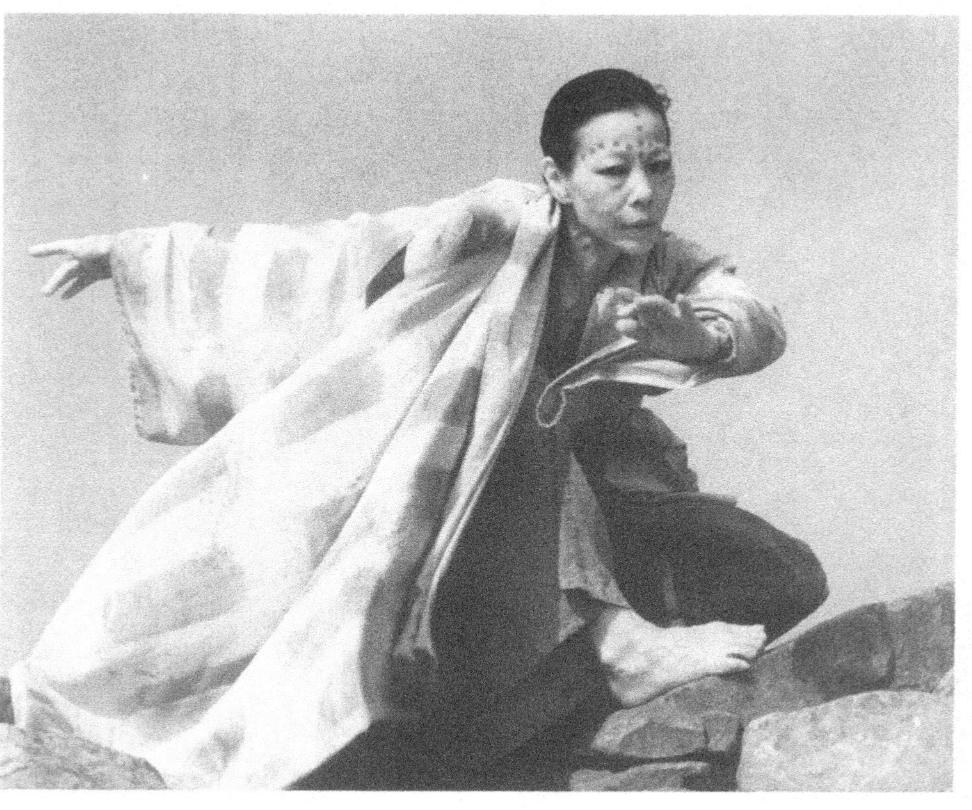

4. I have seen her through the bamboo screen. Artist: Jacqui Chan. Photo: Eric Richmond. Photograph © Pan Project, Holborn Centre, London

the casual, unconcentrated everyday thoughts and movements, and put them into a heightened, free state, echoing the rituals of Hindu culture which do not "make sombre" but which focus and uplift, lightening the individual and the task. This makes "joy" a tangible state, but perhaps one which, in India anyway, cannot be learned by any rules, more by the absorption of a special way of being.

It is difficult to train people in "joy", but it is an atmosphere which, when achieved, can uplift action to a heightened state before creating and before performing. It was in this state that we created Shakti, Sita's Daughters and Itan Kahani, and it works. It is not a set of rules but an attitude which can also be introduced into training, into rehearsal and into a company.

At the end of leading a Kabuki preparation exercise my actors look and feel "charged", focussed and ready. When the neutral mask is mastered, the moment of taking off the mask reveals a face and body free of encumbering anecdote. It is a feeling of latent energy, latent action and the thrill at being in this state.

I am still at it. I need the pre-expressive state, it maximises the actors' expression when it comes. With the studying of energy and precision through many influences, through the study of play as a way of loosening up the specificity of this material and making it flexible, and adding the underlying state of joy in creativity, I see a level in the performer which is more than the everyday: it is heightened, alert, energised and controlled and, what we are all looking for – "ready to go".

Contemporary Theatre Review
1997, Vol. 7, Part 1, pp. 59–60
Reprints available directly from the publisher
Photocopying permitted by license only

Endnote: The Range of Approaches

Ralph Yarrow

The essays in these issues have approached the concepts of presence, pre-expressivity, sub- or underscore and the performative situations in which these occur, from a variety of perspectives. As always, the direction they take yields more in terms of the writer's desired pattern of meaning than in terms of any 'objective' designation. All meaning is tendentious, or to put it less negatively, it is created in our experience as interaction with what we take to be external to us, but which to a large extent is nothing of the kind. Performance itself makes this even more clear since it is a moment-to-moment sequence created by bodies in space-time, whether those bodies are mainly transmitting or mainly receiving information. And investigation of phenomena or conditions as subtle as those dealt with in the essays here must necessarily depend upon the nature of the perceiving and comprehending entity doing the investigating, in other words on the range and quality of its experience.

Agreement then there is not likely to be. Some kinds of consensus are however probable: for a start, there are a number of models or approaches under which the investigations could be grouped:

- biological/physiological: Barba (*bios*), Pradier (energy);
- model of mind or consciousness (Meyer-Dinkgräfe, Yarrow);
- gender (Taylor);
- training/rehearsal (Martin, Pavis);
- process of performance–event (Nicolescu, Chamberlain, Alderson);
- structural investigation (Pavis).

None of these is necessarily waterlight; each could be further divided or categorised. However, these models indicate useful lines of enquiry. What they are enquiring into are the parameters of what Chamberlain has elsewhere called the 'body of the performer', the 'body of the [performance-]text', and the 'body of the audience': that is to say, they are asking how specific and "extra-daily" states come about for these three constituents and how they differ from the everyday.

No single model is likely to prove adequate because the spectrum from presence through pre-expressivity and subscore to the performance–event and its reception encompasses just about any or all facets of what we call creativity; and furthermore Barba's own approach, from which this volume takes its origin, is expressly multi-and/or transcultural and interdisciplinary. There probably cannot be a single method of activating or understanding the complex of events the essays contend with; at best the hope is that writing may be a parallel process of attempting to explore and articulate the experience of heightened functioning. It is important to do so because such 'special situations', with the rapidity of processing and coherence of activity they display, present the possibility of enhancing human functioning as well, perhaps, as facilitating access to the joy of creative acts.

Contemporary Theatre Review
1997, Vol. 7, Part 1, p. 61
Reprints available directly from the publisher
Photocopying permitted by license only

Notes on Contributors

John Martin is artistic director of Pan Project, London's leading intercultural performance company. From a background of Lecoq, Grotowski and LaMama, he has written and directed performances throughout Europe and, in recent years, has collaborated widely with Indian companies and performers. He has also initiated a number of courses on non-western theatre in British universities.

Daniel Meyer-Dinkgräfe studied English, German and Philosophy in Germany. In the summer of 1994 he completed his PhD at the University of London (Royal Holloway) with a thesis on Consciousness and the Actor. Since September 1994 he has lectured in the Department of Theatre, Film and Television Studies at the University of Wales, Aberystwyth.

Basarab Nicolescu is a theoretical physicist, specialising in the theory of elementary particles, at the Centre National de la Recherche Scientifique in Paris. He is the author of numerous scientific articles published in international journals and reviews, as well as being a contributor to a number of research compilations. For a number of years, Dr. Nicolescu has been interested in the relationship between art, science, and traditional thought. In 1968 he published a book discussing the interface between mathematics and poetry. Since 1978, he has been a member of the advisory editorial panel of the interdisciplinary review 3ème Millénaire.

Val Taylor is a theatre director and writer and lectures in Drama at the University of East Anglia.

David Williams teaches performance Studies at the Victoria University, Melbourne, Australia. He has compiled two books on the work of Peter Brook's CICT as well as being a performance maker.

Ralph Yarrow teaches Drama and European Literature at the University of East Anglia. He has published on both areas and on the functioning of consciousness in reception. He directs, performs and adapts for the theatre.

Contemporary Theatre Review
1997, Vol. 7, Part 1, pp. 63–64
Reprints available directly from the publisher
Photocopying permitted by license only

Index

CONTEMPORARY THEATRE REVIEW
AN INTERNATIONAL JOURNAL

Notes for contributors

Submission of a paper will be taken to imply that it represents original work not previously published, that it is not being considered for publication elsewhere and that, if accepted for publication, it will not be published elsewhere in the same form, in any language, without the consent of editor and publisher. It is a condition of acceptance by the editor of a typescript for publication that the publisher automatically acquires the copyright of the typescript throughout the world. It will also be assumed that the author has obtained all necessary permissions to include in the paper items such as quotations, musical examples, figures, tables etc. Permissions should be paid for prior to submission.

Typescripts. Papers should be submitted in triplicate to the Editors, *Contemporary Theatre Review, c/o* Harwood Academic Publishers, at:

5th Floor, Reading Bridge House
Reading Bridge Approach
Reading RGl 8PP
UK

or

820 Town Center Drive
Langhorne
PA 19047 USA

or

3-14-9, Okubo
Shinjuku-ku
Tokyo 169
Japan

Papers should be typed or word processed with double spacing on one side of good quality ISO A4 (212 × 297 mm) paper with a 3 cm left-hand margin. Papers are accepted only in English.

Abstracts and Keywords. Each paper requires an abstract of 100–150 words summarizing the significant coverage and findings, presented on a separate sheet of paper. Abstracts should be followed by up to six key words or phrases which, between them, should indicate the subject matter of the paper. These will be used for indexing and data retrieval purposes.

Figures. All figures (photographs, schema, charts, diagrams and graphs) should be numbered with consecutive arabic numerals, have descriptive captions and be mentioned in the text. Figures should be kept separate from the text but an approximate position for each should be indicated in the margin of the typescript. It is the author's responsibility to obtain permission for any reproduction from other sources.

Preparation: Line drawings must be of a high enough standard for direct reproduction; photocopies are not acceptable. They should be prepared in black (india) ink on white art paper, card or tracing paper, with all the lettering and symbols included. Computer-generated graphics of a similar high quality are also acceptable, as are good sharp photoprints ("glossies"). Computer print-outs must be completely legible. Photographs intended for halftone reproduction must be good glossy original prints of maximum contrast. Redrawing or retouching of unusable figures will be charged to authors.

Size: Figures should be planned so that they reduce to 12 cm column width. The preferred width of line drawings is 24 cm, with capital lettering 4 mm high, for reduction by one-half. Photographs for halftone reproduction should be approximately twice the desired finished size.

Captions: A list of figure captions, with the relevant figure numbers, should be typed on a separate sheet of paper and included with the typescript.

Musical examples: Musical examples should be designated as "Figure 1" etc., and the recommendations above for preparation and sizing should be followed. Examples must be well prepared and of a high standard for reproduction, as they will not be redrawn or retouched by the printer.

In the case of large scores, musical examples will have to be reduced in size and so some clarity will be lost. This should be borne in mind especially with orchestral scores.

Notes are indicated by superior arabic numerals without parentheses. The text of the notes should be collected at the end of the paper.

References are indicated in the text by the name and date system either "Recent work (Smith & Jones, 1987, Robinson, 1985, 1987) . . ." or "Recently Smith & Jones (1987) . . ." If a publication has more than three authors, list all names on the first occurrence; on subsequent occurrences use the first author's name plus "*et al.*" Use an ampersand rather than "and" between the last two authors. If there is more than one publication by the same author(s) in the same year, distinguish by adding a, b, c etc. to both the text citation and the list of references (e.g. "Smith, 1986a") References should be collected and typed in alphabetical order after the Notes and Acknowledgements sections (if these exist). Examples:

Benedetti, J. (1988) *Stanislavski,* London: Methuen

Granville-Barker, H. (1934) Shakespeare's dramatic art. In *A Companion to Shakespeare Studies,* edited by H. Granville-Barker and G. B. Harrison, p. 84. Cambridge: Cambridge University Press

Johnston, D. (1970) Policy in theatre. *Hibernia,* **16**, 16

Proofs. Authors will receive page proofs (including figures) by air mail for correction and these must be returned as instructed within 48 hours of receipt. Please ensure that a full postal address is given on the first page of the typescript so that proofs are not delayed in the post. Authors' alterations, other than those of a typographical nature, in excess of 10% of the original composition cost, will be charged to authors.

Page Charges. There are no page charges to individuals or institutions.

INSTRUCTIONS FOR AUTHORS

ARTICLE SUBMISSION ON DISK

The Publisher welcomes submissions on disk. The instructions that follow are intended for use by authors whose articles have been accepted for publication and are in final form. Your adherence to these guidelines will facilitate the processing of your disk by the typesetter. These instructions do not replace the journal Notes for Contributors; all information in Notes for Contributors remains in effect.

When typing your article, do not include design or formatting information. Type all text flush left, unjustified and without hyphenation. Do not use indents, tabs or multi-spacing. If an indent is required, please note it by a line space; also mark the position of the indent on the hard copy manuscript. Indicate the beginning of a new paragraph by typing a line space. Leave one space at the end of a sentence, after a comma or other punctuation mark, and before an opening parenthesis. Be sure not to confuse lower case letter "l" with numeral "1", or capital letter "O" with numeral "0". Distinguish opening quotes from close quotes. Do not use automatic page numbering or running heads.

Tables and displayed equations may have to be rekeyed by the typesetter from your hard copy manuscript. Refer to the journal Notes for Contributors for style for Greek characters, variables, vectors, etc.

Articles prepared on most word processors are acceptable. If you have imported equations and/or scientific symbols into your article from another program, please provide details of the program used and the procedures you followed. If you have used macros that you have created, please include them as well.

You may supply illustrations that are available in an electronic format on a separate disk. Please clearly indicate on the disk the file format and/or program used to produce them, and supply a high-quality hard copy of each illustration as well.

Submit your disk when you submit your final hard copy manuscript. The disk file and hard copy must match exactly.

If you are submitting more than one disk, please number each disk. Please mark each disk with the journal title, author name, abbreviated article title and file names.

Be sure to retain a back-up copy of each disk submitted. Pack your disk carefully to avoid damage in shipping, and submit it with your hard copy manuscript and complete Disk Specifications form (see reverse) to the person designated in the journal Notes for Contributors.

Disk Specifications

Journal name ______________________________

____

Date ______________ **Paper Reference Number** ______________

Paper title ______________________________

____

____

Corresponding author ______________________________

Address ______________________________

____

____

______________________________ **Postcode** ______________

Telephone ______________________________

Fax ______________________________

E-mail ______________________________

Disks Enclosed (file names and descriptions of contents)

Text

Disk 1 ______________________________

Disk 2 ______________________________

Disk 3 ______________________________

PLEASE RETAIN A BACK-UP COPY OF ALL DISK FILES SUBMITTED.

Figures

Disk 1 ________________________________

Disk 2 ________________________________

Disk 3 ________________________________

Computer make and model ________________________

____

Size/format of floppy disks

☐ 3.5" ☐ 5.25"

☐ Single sided ☐ Double sided

☐ Single density ☐ Double density ☐ High density

Operating system ____________________________

Version ________________________________

Word processor program ________________________

Version ________________________________

Imported maths/science program ____________________

Version ________________________________

Graphics program ____________________________

Version ________________________________

Files have been saved in the following format

Text: ________________________________

Figures: ______________________________

Maths: _______________________________

PLEASE RETAIN A BACK-UP COPY OF ALL DISK FILES SUBMITTED.

For Product Safety Concerns and Information please contact our EU representative GPSR@taylorandfrancis.com
Taylor & Francis Verlag GmbH, Kaufingerstraße 24, 80331 München, Germany

www.ingramcontent.com/pod-product-compliance
Lightning Source LLC
LaVergne TN
LVHW010942110826
845149LV00013B/2716

* 9 7 8 9 0 5 7 0 2 1 7 5 6 *